Creativity Diagnostics

Heribert Wienkamp

Creativity Diagnostics

Springer

Heribert Wienkamp
Recklinghausen, Germany

ISBN 978-3-662-70431-8 ISBN 978-3-662-70432-5 (eBook)
https://doi.org/10.1007/978-3-662-70432-5

Translation from the German language edition: "Kreativitätsdiagnostik" by Heribert Wienkamp, © Der/die Herausgeber bzw. der/die Autor(en), exklusiv lizenziert an Springer-Verlag GmbH, DE, ein Teil von Springer Nature 2025. Published by Springer Berlin Heidelberg. All Rights Reserved.

This book is a translation of the original German edition "Kreativitätsdiagnostik" by Heribert Wienkamp, published by Springer-Verlag GmbH, DE in 2024. The translation was done with the help of an artificial intelligence machine translation tool. A subsequent human revision was done primarily in terms of content, so that the book will read stylistically differently from a conventional translation. Springer Nature works continuously to further the development of tools for the production of books and on the related technologies to support the authors.

This Springer imprint is published by the registered company Springer-Verlag GmbH, DE, part of Springer Nature.
The registered company address is: Heidelberger Platz 3, 14197 Berlin, Germany

Preface

Creativity diagnostics is without a doubt a "difficult business" and presents almost insurmountable challenges to every practitioner. By no means do grand ideas flow easily in this task, and a "know-how" does not automatically emerge. Based on previous publications, it can be assumed that many attempts have already been made to assess creativity, for example, through specially developed creativity tests. With the exception of pieces of work or work samples from the artistic-scientific milieu to determine "creative" talents, it has neither been conclusively achieved in educational diagnostics for schoolchildren nor in corporate personnel selection or professional aptitude diagnostics to master these methodological requirements and to develop suitable or—even better—optimal procedures or instruments.

Given this initial situation, it is understandably difficult for any author to confront this problem and take on the methodological challenge in order to set new accents in creativity diagnostics. I myself have also long considered how a useful contribution in the form of a specialist book could turn out, without merely "simply and bluntly" repeating the findings and procedures published so far or similar!

It is simply a fact that creativity is not only an ominous and dazzling term but also represents a personality trait that cannot be prescribed and established under comparable conditions. "Be spontaneous" is just as ineffective as "be creative"! Under these conditions, standardized procedures like tests can only fail, so it is a wonder that creativity tests have nevertheless been constructed and exist as diagnostic instruments. Therefore, the purpose of this contribution is not to present a new creativity test or similar as a *standardized* instrument, but to highlight other possibilities of creativity diagnostics that could also be conceivable in occupational aptitude diagnostics. Undoubtedly, an important concern in this context is to point out that there is not one single or *the* approach, but rather it is important to "let the mind wander" and systematically expand the diagnostic framework. Perhaps a more playfully constructed and conducted procedure can also come closer to creativity (see Appendix 2).

As a solution and an option, on the one hand, the application of scenarios of "open problems" is offered, which, however, should be well prepared both methodically with the help of special and suitable assessment grids and by prior exploration of the expected answers or solutions. Scenarios differ from strictly regulated procedures like tests by the rather informal approach to the open problems, which the candidate attempts to solve through questions and answers to themselves and is observed and assessed by a "jury." On the other hand, the diagnostician should not "stare like a rabbit at a snake" only at creativity or focus solely on it as a characteristic, but should simultaneously keep an eye on the "nosological network" of personality traits corresponding with creativity and aim to create a profile of characteristics.

Another possibility would be not only to search for creative behavior in a positive sense, but instead to turn to a "negative diagnostics" in order to diagnose, for example, rigid or inflexible behavior, which very likely means the opposite of creativity and becomes particularly noticeable within social relationships. Especially in social relationships, it sometimes depends on imagination, empathy, and intuition, which are revealed in social understanding and the consciously chosen or involuntary reactions, for example, in the request for feedback. Unfortunately, not everyone possesses or masters these "social skills" to a sufficient degree.

Not only for social relationships, in addition to the production of good ideas and solutions to the problems at hand, is mental flexibility and the ability to combine required, which positively and creatively manifests itself in the effective use of mental and diverse assessment schemes or category systems. In contrast to intelligence diagnostics, in creativity diagnostics, there is not one correct solution, but usually, many alternatives are available to choose from.

In the age of social media, social resonance in the public sphere also plays an increasingly significant role in creative ideas or works, which, in their impact through dissemination on the internet or in social networks, and in their usefulness as feedback to the (creative) initiator, should not be underestimated.

It remains to be hoped that this reading contains and presents some suggestions and alternatives for creativity diagnostics that could noticeably assist you as a personnel manager and evaluator of individuals.

Recklinghausen
in January 2024

Dr. Heribert Wienkamp

Contents

Introduction

1

Some, if not many, people doubt that creativity diagnostics can be accomplished at all. For creativity diagnostics is a paradox or a contradiction in itself, as no person can be creative on command! "Be spontaneous" works just as little in communication and interaction among people, as we all know, as the command: Be creative!

Creativity and intelligence sometimes seem like "Siamese twins," which complement each other and somehow belong together, but do not unite or merge, instead remaining independent mental achievements. Thus, there is no way around dealing with intelligence research or the diagnostics of mental performances and processes when discussing creativity, or specifically creativity diagnostics.

Much has already been said and written about intelligence, and as a result of scientific research, a number of intelligence models exist that differ and distinguish themselves in their structures and in their diversity of components or in their functions. Thus, it is not presumptuous to say that there is not the intelligence concept per se, but rather many—which is also not a novelty in scientific research!

Even vaguer, or even "fuzzier," is the concept of creativity. For some researchers, it is a part or subfactor of intelligence, associated with inspiration, insight (English: insight), or inventiveness or creativity (e.g., as a defined intelligence performance in the "Berlin Intelligence Structure Test" by Jäger et al., 1997; see also Sect. 4.1.2). Other authors (see Guilford, 1964; cited in Preiser, 1976, p. 55) describe creativity as "divergent thinking" (as a counterpart or contrast to "convergent thinking") or also "inferential thinking" (see e.g., Schuler & Görlich, 2007, p. 20 ff.), when the aspect of synthesis ability in problem-solving with the help or application of new ideas is particularly prominent. Sternberg (1985) contrasted "inductive reasoning" with "deductive reasoning" as fluid abilities that lead to ideas or solutions, which is related to the thought process starting either "bottom-up" or "top-down." New ideas do not automatically lead to "brilliant" solutions by themselves, but they must be connectable and integrate with existing experiential knowledge, making them context-dependent.

H. Wienkamp, *Creativity Diagnostics*, https://doi.org/10.1007/978-3-662-70432-5_1

Puristically viewed, a creation or a creative product would be something that has not existed before or has never been there. But: In our world, creativity is understood as something that emerges from the existing and develops into something new. This applies equally to mental (like ideas or thoughts) as well as material (like products or objects) creations. Creative achievements are thus new to us as directly affected individuals, but not necessarily for all people in this world, as Barron (1965, p. 3 ff.) highlighted in his review.

The concept of creativity can be further expanded if it is understood as a "social and cultural product" whose development is only granted to humans. However, it is also clear that such a universal understanding of creative achievements created by "human hands" (or creativity as a trait) increasingly distances itself from the concern and determination or diagnostics of creativity. Such an opinion or approach appeals to authors (see e.g., the anthology by Neves-Pereira & Pinheiro, 2023) who view creativity as a general human trait or characteristic closely linked to an individual's life history and finds its origin therein. Against the backdrop of humanity, this statement is understandable and comprehensible!—Or put differently: If every person can or is creative only in their own way, why should we then try to determine or objectify creativity? Perhaps only to capture and identify different degrees of creativity, that is, to quantify or measure it? And what would be the point if creativity or the quality of creative achievements can only be judged individually and thus not directly comparable? Many questions that demand serious answers!

However, it is not the case that the attempt to conduct creativity diagnostics has never been made in scientific psychology. Some creativity tests in professional aptitude diagnostics, as well as work samples, e.g., as proof of suitability or talent for studying at an art college, may provide evidence for this. Not to mention the efforts with preschool or school children to determine creative performances or talents, which were not particularly successful under certain situational conditions (see e.g., Seiffge-Krenke, 1974).

In dealing with creativity diagnostics, it is essential to first closely examine the relationship between intelligence and creativity or to devote oneself to intelligence research with its different models and diagnostic procedures. Then it is necessary to turn to the construct of "creativity" with the aim of determining and describing its independence as a mental or cognitive performance, in order to find initial or further research approaches. In the professional context or in the working world, the distinction from the characteristic "innovation capacity" plays a particularly important role. Finally, the special situation in job-related creativity diagnostics must be addressed to indicate the limits and perspectives or prospects of success for any kind of creativity diagnostics—or not!

In conclusion, an "excursion" or a foray into the "social reality" of human interactions and relationships is needed before addressing the embedding of creativity diagnostics in general personality diagnostics. As will be shown, creative approaches are indeed helpful in truly understanding other individuals in their current situation and in handling and successfully managing a range of social matters and phenomena.

2 Intelligence Research and Intelligence Models

According to the opinion of many scientists and in view of their existing findings, intelligence is an important prerequisite for initiating and developing something like problem-solving ability—or even creativity, where the designation fits and is appropriate. Research results from relevant studies on creative achievements showed correlative relationships of a medium or moderate size around $r = 0.30$, thus indicating a statistically significant connection between the evaluated creative achievements and the total score of an intelligence test. Since, as a rule, the individual intelligence factors also stood in a positive correlative relationship with each other of approximately comparable size and expression, it can be assumed that a whole bundle of intellectual abilities generated the correlative connection to creativity, although the influence of individual intelligence factors was controversial in research and sparked lively discussions.

Perhaps it makes sense, therefore, to gradually and stepwise introduce intelligence as a mental performance and in this sequence address the existing insights into the sizes of intelligence as causes of mental performances along with their theories and models.

It should be mentioned in advance that for every theory or psychological construct, it is necessary to clarify the contents to establish face validity as a thematic framework for further empirical investigations. This works best through surveys of both laypeople and experts about what they generally understand by intelligence and which specific mental processes they attribute to intelligence. According to statements from intelligence research, experts and laypeople are quite in agreement when asked about their view and opinion of an "ideal" intelligent person, as indicated by the high correlation measures (see Sternberg, 1985, p. 64).

In contrast to these implicit theories, which are more a matter of opinion about intelligence or intelligent people as projections, scientific intelligence research is increasingly dedicated to uncovering intelligence structures and causative factors as (or for) intelligence performances and uses empirical investigations with subsequent objective mathematical-statistical evaluation to verify their (explicit)

H. Wienkamp, *Creativity Diagnostics*, https://doi.org/10.1007/978-3-662-70432-5_2

theories and models. A popular evaluation tool is factor analysis (see, for example, Tabachnick & Fidell, 2007, as a representative of multivariate statistical methods), which searches through the diversity of individual and test results for so-called main components as causes and identifies them as such, making their existence dependent on the extent to which they can explain the variability or variance in the test results and assign them to defined intelligence factors. Depending on the question, there are independent operationalizations in which the search direction reveals itself depending on the model-theoretical considerations such as assumptions or hypotheses.

2.1 Overview of Classical Intelligence Models and Intelligence Factors

Initially, there were different ideas in psychology about what intelligence means and constitutes when the rather banal view that intelligence is what an intelligence test measures does not apply and is ignored. All psychometrically derived intelligence models are more or less the result of factor analyses that decomposed the event space of test results into influence or causative factors, i.e., intelligence factors.

An earlier approach assumed a general factor (g) for intelligence, which produces the mental energy for intellectual cognitive performances and is responsible for the activities in various subfactors of intelligence. These subfactors include, for example, 1) reading and comprehension, 2) verbal fluency in the use of language, 3) numerical understanding and calculations, 4) spatial visualization ability, etc.

A completely different model proceeded "bottom-up" instead of "top-down" and oriented itself to the mental qualities and processes by breaking down mental performances according to results, contents, and operations, which in Guilford's model (1964; cited in Preiser, 1976, p. 54 ff.) later led to 120 "activity cells" of mental abilities and activities. For a large part of these activity cells, empirical evidence could also be provided from research and practice. Subsequent factor analyses led to the extraction of main factors of intelligent performances such as 1) memory performances, 2) convergent thinking for drawing logical conclusions as the only correct or obvious result for judgments and decisions, 3) divergent thinking for generating new thoughts, creative ideas, and associations from existing information with several possible solution alternatives, 4) evaluations for reflections and controls, and 5) other cognitions such as perceptions, imaginations, etc.

Other models of intelligence were satisfied with coarser structures or classifications, such as a differentiation between verbal-knowledge-based intelligence and practical-technical intelligence or between "fluid" and "crystalline" intelligence with their divergent independent functions and processes.

Fluid intelligence represents inductive thinking, which is supposed to lead to or contribute to logical conclusions. Colloquially, this mental activity can also be translated or described with the solution of "brain teasers." Often, certain conditions or premises are given in the test tasks, e.g., a number series with the sequence 3, 6, 9, etc., which follows a certain rule that the test subject has to derive from a selection of alternatives and complete the number series with the next (correct or right) element.

Fluid intelligence also includes deductive reasoning. Such mental activities require "abstraction skills," by concluding from individual parts to the "big picture," for example, through summaries or classifications, which could be referred to as categorization or structure formation, to establish a connection between element and category. Likewise, linear transformations fall under this, such as (A > B) and (B > C) = > (A > C), as well as conditional conditions and derivations, for example, in the form of "if-then statements."

Crystalline intelligence, on the other hand, is dedicated to the use of language and understanding texts. It is either about the "art of learning vocabulary" or deciphering the provided clues from text passages with unknown words to infer the possible meaning of the new unknown word. To keep track of these many models and submodels or facets of intelligence (from the already cited specialized literature), reference is made to Table 2.1 as an aid.

Other models assume a genetically determined component of intelligence in competition with a cultural-social influence (see e.g. Wewetzer, 1984).

Of the individual qualities of intelligence, the problem-solving ability, which is so important and decisive in practice, is likely to depend. However, complicated or complex problem-solving requires a dedicated and disciplined process if it is to be effective and sustainable in the long term. For more clarity and transparency, a "process model" of cognitive performances and processes can provide, which follows the following sequences:

1) Perception and recognition of whether there is a problem to be solved at all, and if so, what type of problem it is. Tackling "pseudo-problems" or attempting to solve the "wrong problems" has never worked and is a pure waste of time and resources.
2) Complex problems require careful analysis according to, for example, "cause-effect" or, as in medicine, according to disease and symptoms (or in the diagnostic process exactly the other way around). Only when all details, relationships, and ramifications are openly "on the table" can the search for a solution begin.
3) Summaries, categorizations, or exclusion of elements as mental abstractions result in an action strategy that follows certain target ideas. Action goals are then the product of synthesis ability and provide a solution path as a sequence of partial steps, i.e., what is to be done now and next, which would generally be referred to as an action strategy. Sometimes, experimenting through "trial-error behavior" and the "view from above" or the whole ("the big picture") is necessary and required.
4) Since errors or mistakes can never be completely ruled out during the action process, process control and self-reflection must take place at the end—preferably through plausibility checks or, if possible, through external feedback.

Table 2.1 Schema for classifying selected thinking styles as facets of intelligence

No.	Model or Design	Example	Note
1	General factor—Subfactors	Intelligence quotient (IQ) vs. e.g., memory performance	Several subfactors make up the general factor
2	Analytical—Inferential thinking	Detail-oriented investigations and evaluations vs. Synthesis formation	It applies: Thesis + Antithesis = Synthesis
3	Fluid (liquid)—Crystalline intelligence	"Brain teasers" vs. Vocabulary learning	Logical reasoning versus language applications (exegeses) with necessary prior knowledge
4	Inductive—Deductive thinking	Finding solutions and making decisions vs. Abstractions through integration (class formation) and transformations (e.g., "if, then")	Direction: once "bottom-up," on the other "top-down"
5	Divergent—Convergent thinking	Idea generation vs. Review and evaluation	Divergent thinking = multidimensional thinking or creativity (?)
6	Linguistic-knowledge-based—Practical-technical intelligence	Learning from new information plus (pre-) knowledge vs. Application of know-how ("knowing how")	Linking old and new as well as transfer to new problems
7	Social—Pragmatic intelligence	Dealing with people in social situations vs. Tactical skill	Subjective experience compared to the situational-object-related "world"

2.2 Further Models

Not only the "classical" intelligence models shape the current state of intelligence research. In addition to these historical concepts, new approaches now and repeatedly provide additional insights that apparently researched more "behind the scenes" and relied, among other things, on metacognitions. Metacognitions could clarify or demonstrate as correlations previously hidden connections and links between the intelligence factors as predictors or independent variables (IV) and the observable intelligence performances or test results as dependent variables (DV).

But not only these intervening variables as mediators shape the events according to current ideas, but also entirely different factors must be considered in the context of mental performances or comparable matters, which are not necessarily attributable to cognitive or mental information and processing processes. Rather, they originate from the emotional or emotional experience background, i.e., the *"emotional memory,"* which, parallel to the mental processing processes, equally contribute to judgment formation or decision-making in significant situations or difficult problem constellations. Intuition, hedonistic influences, and the use of both cognitive heuristics and affect-related decision bases such as the *"affect heuristic"* by Slovic et al. (2009) are the decisive psychological mechanisms for this.

2.2.1 Metacognitions as Mediators

Metacognitions support manifest cognitive or mental performances through predictions, planning, control (or monitoring), imagination or imaginations, elaborations through, for example, experimenting in the sense of "trial and error," and controls for self-checking or reflection, as particularly noted by Sternberg (1985, pp. 23 and 80 ff.).

In metacognitions, general intelligence is reflected, which particularly determines *"coping,"* namely to manage new challenges or problems with the available means or resources and thus to deal with them successfully (which could also be understood and referred to as *resilience*)—unlike when dealing with already known tasks, where expertise, skill through practice, and speed show as performance and success criteria (cf. Sternberg, 1985, p. 77).

It is often assumed that metacognitions benefit from the subconscious and find support through insights, inspirations (as new ideas), or mental leaps. Similar to the findings from Gestalt psychology, perspective changes, attitude changes, or the like can create new other shapes or figures against the existing background (which would be the experiential knowledge). However, it is controversial to what extent these theoretical assumptions are verifiable (see Sternberg, 1985, pp. 79 f.).

According to Sternberg (1985), the functionalities of metacognitions include:

(1) decoding, namely separating important from unimportant or irrelevant information;
(2) selective combining, to give details a deeper meaning together with other information and to integrate them into a coherent picture; for example, in medicine, not just one symptom leads to a diagnosis, but often several symptoms;
(3) selective comparisons of new insights with existing knowledge (i.e., "old knowledge") increase know-how and are what constitutes expertise.

With the help of these cognitive or mental operations, an individual derives what constitutes a successful action strategy, which inspires them and can rely on planning and control and on decisions based on correct, reality-based judgments in their concrete behavior. It should also be considered that new knowledge is not yet a guarantee for successful task completion or problem-solving if these metacognitions are inadequately developed or do not function appropriately (cf. Sternberg, 1985, p. 110).

Whether metacognitions influence intellectual performance, for example, represented in school grades as success criteria (or DV), can be methodically examined through a "multiple linear regression analysis (MLRA)" according to the approach of Barron and Kenny (1986) for investigating moderator or mediator effects. In this methodological concept, as in any MLRA, certain predictors are present as independent influencing factors (or IV). On the other hand, in line with the model for the possible influence of intervening variables, there are, on one hand, *moderators* (e.g., gender or age). Moderators gradually determine the influence of the IV on the DV, for example, if older schoolchildren tend to achieve better test results than younger schoolchildren. *Mediators* are, on the other hand, the psychological constructs acting in the background (such as exam or test anxiety), which can exert a dominant influence and are to be detected through theoretical or hypothetical assumptions (such as hypotheses).

Independent predictors (as IV) can, according to an example by Barron and Kenny (1986), in this model, be an instruction as a learning aid with the experimental variant *"yes"* or *"no"*, the dependent outcome or criterion variable, for example, the result in points in a performance test. As intervening variables, once the affiliation to a social class, such as a child *with* or *without* a migration background, was considered as a moderator, and on the other hand, exam anxiety as a psychological construct, which was to be measured, for example, through a personality test with the feature scale "exam anxiety." Sometimes it may happen that the influence on the dependent variable "result in the performance test" depends solely on the negative influence of the mediator "exam anxiety," and when controlling for this intervening variable, the influence of the predictor "learning aid yes or no" becomes statistically insignificant or even tends towards zero.

Metacognitions are also associated with mediators, which moderate the influence of one or more independent variables, such as vocabulary knowledge in a foreign language or reading comprehension in a text with unknown words, which is evident in text exegeses with a hermeneutic background and can be determined. The influence of these independent variables on a criterion variable such as the school grade could possibly be overlaid and moderated by metacognitions, which would need to be diagnosed.

Metacognitions gain effectiveness, for example, through decoding or discovering important information or when combining this new information by establishing abstract connections and, for example, deciphering their meaning through cause-effect mechanisms (also with the help of currently known "if-then statements"). Finally, the newly gained insights should be compared with existing knowledge and, as far as possible, checked for plausibility. Together with the other variables IV and DV, the extent of the metacognitions should be operationalized and captured and presented within the framework of an overall model, and the individual effects on the DV should be calculated.

As a result of such an analysis, it could be found:

a) The mediator variable (or here the metacognitions) has no influence on the external or success criterion (e.g., the school grade).
b) The mediator exerts a partial influence on the criterion variable or the success criterion if the regression coefficients of the IV (e.g., vocabulary knowledge) become smaller and lose weight, so that the mediator as metacognition acquires and has a possibly statistically significant influence on the DV.
c) The mediator or the metacognitions exert a total influence on the success criterion as DV, so that the independent predictors no longer exert a statistically significant or even no influence at all, and the mediator variable alone contributes to explaining the variance.

It is easy to determine that the metacognitions described here directly relate to the sub-steps or sequences in the "process model of intellectual performance" (see Sect. 2.1) and enrich and underpin the actions with specific cognitive inputs as abilities for general problem-solving.

Whether "practical intelligence," as outlined by Sternberg (1985, p. 267 ff.), shows a certain proximity to metacognitions is a matter of opinion. It is certain that this form of intelligence did not significantly correlate with intelligence quotients (IQ) and derives and transfers its know-how or "know-how" from other contexts or areas of life. Most often, "practical intelligence" (here called "pragmatic intelligence"; see Table 2.1) was demonstrated through very intimate and precise knowledge of the relevant area of life, such as the professional or working world, where "tactical skill" was successfully applied to newly arisen problems.

2.2.2 Affective Influences on New Problems

In addition to cognitive factors, alongside metacognitions for special intellectual performances, emotional or affective influences also act as "input providers" in many problem-solving attempts. They provide the individual with a feeling-dependent orientation as a decision-making or action aid in many critical situations, which is gladly used in case of doubt.

In research, the term *intuition* or *"intuitive intelligence"* is used when emotional impulses are meant in behavioral reactions. In common parlance, terms like "having a good nose" or "gut feeling," which manifests as an inherent feeling in important decisions, are used. All in all, feelings accompany the decision-making or behavioral process and provide this process with important orientation. Emotional sensations are particularly evident when a "good" idea suddenly reaches consciousness, and after the euphoria, a deep relieving relaxation occurs, which is experienced as very pleasant.

Also, *heuristics* as so-called rules of thumb are occasionally or frequently used as orientation aids in decisions or problem-solving when other behaviorally relevant information is lacking. Heuristics are based on experiential knowledge from the past, and the decision-maker is guided by what seems familiar or known to him. On the other hand, the alternative favored by the application of the heuristic also reflects the intuition or gut feeling of the affected person, which he follows involuntarily. Heuristics and intuition originate from the "emotional memory" or are parts of it.

In not all cases is success guaranteed in intuitive decisions or reactions. As research has shown (see e.g., Kahneman, 2012), hedonistic influences also play a role in emotion-driven reactions, which obey completely different psychological mechanisms. For example, convenience or "mental laziness" is mentioned in this context, both in thinking and acting, as a preferred influencer that leads to mental shortcuts and thus also to errors in behavior. Responsible for this is *"System 1,"* which follows certain hedonistic impulses in a spontaneous way, without thinking much about the situation, and suggests actions that then turn out to be wrong or faulty. When *"System 2"* is activated as the slower but more thorough cognitive system, which relies on analyses and examination procedures, these shortcuts of "System 1," uncovered by "System 2," are then revealed as errors or human weaknesses.

A commonly chosen example comes from roulette: If the same color (e.g., red) appears in several consecutive rounds, a player is inclined to instinctively and involuntarily bet on the other color (black) in the next game, because he mistakenly assumes it is now due and will most likely appear. Such misconceptions are owed to "System 1" with its spontaneity, as "System 2" would rightly point out that the probability for a game color in each round remains equally high at 0.50.

Decision situations are sometimes opaque and fraught with much uncertainty. A possible reaction would be to "push the ambivalence to the extreme" through the mechanism of "affect heuristic" (see e.g., Slovic et al., 2009) and proceed according to a consciously simple scheme, namely either "good" or "bad" or "do" or "do not ." The affect heuristic is an "artificial" abstraction process that reduces a complex or opaque problem to a simple alternative evaluation that leads to action or decision.

One thing should be mentioned and clarified in this context: The "emotional intelligence" that roams in popular science literature has little or (almost) nothing to do with intuition in this cognitive-affective sense, but is only used in interpersonal or social interactions. For example, it is "emotionally more intelligent" not to say everything to a conversation partner or acquaintance that one thinks and would later regret.

2.3 Summary

There are intelligence models in a wide variety of structures and diversity that allow and facilitate the assignment of individual qualitative performances. Factor analyses were predominantly involved in the model structures as an evaluation method, which decomposed the empirical test results into main components and bundled the variability in the individual results into intelligence factors. Known intelligence factors include, for example, fluid intelligence for inductive (fluid) thinking and reasoning, and crystallized intelligence, which is responsible for the knowledge stored in memory (such as vocabulary) and for acquiring new information, such as learning new vocabulary in a foreign language.

A structuring as a process model is also helpful for understanding intelligence and its practical application.

Metacognitions have been able to enrich intelligence research and uncover and identify the causative factors of intelligent performances operating behind the scenes (metacognitions as mediators). Their most important functions are decoding information, selective combining, and selective comparing, from which new insights arise. People who master the application of metacognitions are more successful in coping with new challenges and problems by using their natural strengths and talents and more easily find an appropriate goal-oriented action strategy. Coping in this sense is therefore closely linked to resilience.

That feelings or affects accompany intelligence processes is a matter of course. In case of doubt, they provide individuals with orientation in opaque decision-making situations. Intuition or "intuitive intelligence," for example, originates from the "gut feeling" and is physically perceptible.

Heuristics as "rules of thumb" or similar also provide orientation in unclear situations and offer active assistance in behavior, as individuals can access their familiar experiences or their stored knowledge in memory.

However, the use of heuristics should not be confused with hedonistic influences, which can lead the affected individuals astray if they succumb to these temptations, for example, out of mental laziness or convenience. Cognitive-emotional influences also include the "affect heuristic," which encourages and tempts the decision-maker to engage in "black-and-white thinking" in order to make a decision at all based on their experiences stored in the "emotional memory." It would be completely out of place to speak of "emotional intelligence" in the context of cognitive processes.

Creativity 3

Creativity is in demand as a psychological trait in many situations, whether at work or at home with problems in private life. Certainly, everyone strives for creative solutions to new unknown problems or assumes that they possess this trait if they succeeded in overcoming the not necessarily easy new challenges and received positive feedback from others.

Creativity was and still is a difficult terrain in psychological research. It was only with Guilford (1950) and his then sensational contribution, which "put the finger on the wound" and lamented the until then greatly neglected creativity research, that creativity research gained momentum. Apparently, scientific psychology had so far overlooked that creativity depends on certain personality traits, which every person possesses to varying degrees. According to this understanding, creative behavior arises with the help of a specific pattern of traits, regardless of the discipline or domain (and perhaps with the exception of genius achievements in art). It would also be wrong to understand that high intelligence alone generates creativity and that the study of creativity would already be completed with intelligence research.

What makes the study of creativity so difficult, however, is its spontaneous, unplanned occurrence, when it appears like "force majeure" or as a sudden event. Moreover, its manifestation is not solely situation-dependent, but also person- and time-dependent. This means nothing other than that a person can be creative in a certain situation, but in another, albeit similar or comparable situation, they may not be and may lack any creativity.

Anyone who speaks of creativity must also say what they understand by it, and therefore cannot avoid an appropriate definition or understanding. In psychological research, the concepts of creativity, which is no wonder or great surprise, are not uniform. *Originality, usefulness*, and *acceptance* are considered the general criteria for new proposals or ideas, on which most experts have now been able to agree.

H. Wienkamp, *Creativity Diagnostics*, https://doi.org/10.1007/978-3-662-70432-5_3

Creativity, as a personality construct, very likely also requires support or "flanking protection" from other character traits, such as self-confidence or risk-taking, if it is to be fully effective. Only a more detailed analysis can help, determining what corresponds with the trait of creativity and is absolutely necessary for the emergence of creativity, such as a certain level of basic intelligence, and what is conducive to creativity, such as curiosity and self-confidence. Ideally, a theory or model performs this work of clarifying the relationship to other psychological traits, including operationalization (see also Chaps. 4 and 7). Therefore, there is no way around getting closer to the personality traits (including intelligence) of creativity as a model or construct and conducting empirical investigations, regardless of how the relevant personality traits relate to each other and whether they correlate. Some traits or abilities will have a close relationship to an individual's creativity, others rather not and tend towards zero or do not correlate. Such a pattern of relationships was already prevalent and typical for the intelligence factors both among themselves and to the overall intelligence, measured by the intelligence quotient (IQ).

But not only the person or personality is at the center of the discussion about creativity. According to the popular concept of the "4 × P's," namely *"person, process, product, press"* by Rhodes (1962; cited in Beghetto & Kaufman, 2022, p. 24), other factors also determine creativity. While the person stands for the favorable personality dispositions, as presented, the process is associated with a chronological sequence or a temporally staggered stage concept from problem identification to problem-solving. Creative products are then the new ideas or proposals, either as "Mini- or Little C's" or as "Big C's," when creativity is associated with normal everyday problems on the one hand, and with spectacular and genius inventions or, for example, grandiose artworks (as the "Big C's") on the other (see e.g., Dow, 2022). "Press" in English stands for the drive through intrinsic motivation to continuously and repeatedly engage with the same problem, as well as for the external pressure from the social environment; therefore, a German synonym for "P" could be the (interested) "public."

Finally, it is necessary to "get good creative ideas off the ground," which then leads to proper innovation management in the corporate working world. However, this presupposes acting persons or actors who have sufficient innovative capacity, paired with a sense of reality or feasibility thinking, to transform these creative ideas into suitable projects or prototypes and develop them to market maturity.

3.1 Creativity as a Personality Construct

Creativity is indeed a dazzling term and for various reasons "on everyone's lips," but unfortunately, the concepts of it are vague and imprecise. Science and practice can most agree that creativity is not needed for standard problems, even if they should be difficult and demanding in execution, but only for new extraordinary problems, for which a person can neither prepare nor equip themselves well, nor do ideal solutions immediately emerge in the vague. It seems undisputed, therefore, that creativity is not something completely new, but it does bring forth new things like new ideas, products, theories, etc., and it is new for the interested audience. For the original creative idea to stand out from the "original nonsense" (Preiser, 1976, p. 3), the creative achievement must make sense or have something *useful* about it or provide added value. However, a benefit can only be objectively and consistently assessed by a reference group affected by it, so that creations depend on the "social echo" or the *positive resonance*. High agreement in the assessment of the factual usefulness of a creative idea is simultaneously considered proof of quality, which an "interrater reliability" indicates as an indicator (and expression of a common understanding) (see Hennessey & Amaible, 1988, p. 16).

Inventors or similar, according to Guilford (1950), whose opinion is certainly shared by many other researchers, are not the eager learner type or even nerds, but they have "their own mind," which enables them to think unorthodoxly or behave unconventionally. However, they do need knowledge or prior experience regarding the subject matter, because creativity does not thrive in a vacuum! The outstanding strength of creative people lies in their *transfer skills,* such as recognizing similarities between foreign things or fields and forming analogies.

It cannot be ruled out that creativity bears some similarity to the already presented metacognitions (see Sect. 2.2.1). Metacognitions are characterized by thinking and acting that, so to speak, "go beyond the horizon" in tackling tasks (e.g., in text or puzzle tasks in an intelligence test) and in which *highly* and *limited intelligent* people differ significantly. The explanations of Gestalt psychology about creativity seem to be the most applicable and comprehensible when it comes to the redesign or "reformation" of an incomplete, mismatched "picture" with a collection of arbitrarily accumulated elements. Only when the unordered picture is transformed into a new shape or figure through the creative process and "gives the whole" or the picture *"a face,"* which is more than the sum of its parts, can it be spoken of as a creative achievement (comparable to a puzzle game).

Creativity builds on experiential knowledge, which means: Creativity "does not fall from the sky"! But creative people have the cognitive quality or ability to *"think outside the box,"* to completely question and radically rethink things or developments that were previously seen or understood in a certain (wrong) way. Or another way would be to take an unfamiliar viewpoint and thus see the situation or event differently and indeed give them new meanings. If necessary, a bird's-eye view, that is, from above, would also be an option. That too would be creative!

This aligns with the view that, in addition to the original and many ideas, adaptive flexibility is crucial. Based on earlier studies by Guilford on military officers, who were observed by experienced judges as "interraters" in social situations and also subjected to creativity tests, it was found that the creativity characteristics identified by the observers *Originality, Adaptive Flexibility* and *Fluency of Ideas* moderately correlated with the results in the creativity tests (see, for example, Barron, 1965, p. 41 ff.).

In social relationships, it often depends, and thus is quite comparable to the bird's-eye view, on the design of metacommunication, which, in addition to current problem sensitivity, depends on a *"communicative smoothness"* (Wienkamp, 2021a, p. 15) with creative approaches to be effective (see Chap. 5).

In creativity efforts, there can be the "brilliant idea" that comes more or less spontaneously and suddenly strikes a person as an *"Aha experience."* However, creativity can also mean *"drilling thick boards,"* when individuals repeatedly engage with the same thought or problem and only after many attempts or "trial-and-error actions" find the right way to solve the problem or at least get an idea of the direction in which they need to search (as Hennessey & Amaible, 1988, p. 19, have already pointed out in the past).

In the scientific research literature, creativity as a personality trait was also frequently the focus. Thus, creativity researchers conducted extreme group comparisons between, on the one hand, *"creative individuals"* and, on the other hand, *"non-creative individuals"*. With a selected profile of different personality traits, they hoped to find statistically significant differences in the personality traits (see, for example, the personality profile based on regression coefficients of identified traits of creative individuals by Cattel et al.; cited in Schuler & Görlich, 2007, pp. 12 ff.). Other creativity studies dealt with correlation analyses and primarily related creative achievements to intelligence (see Sect. 3.2). Correlation calculations, like factor analyses (see Sect. 2.1), do not provide causal conclusions and justifications, but only establish patterns of relationships.

It should not be surprising that creativity was often correlated with intelligence or intelligence factors. However, correlations between these two cognitive performances are sample-dependent, i.e., in a random sample with *mixed intelligence* subjects, relatively high correlations up to $r = 0.70$ were found, whereas the correlation coefficients tended towards zero in a group of *highly intelligent* individuals. For the gifted, intelligence no longer contributes any additional value or benefit to the realization of creative achievements (see Preiser, 1976, p. 52), because simply all subjects were highly intelligent and there was no variance in this trait—and consequently no correlation as a measure of relationship!

While in intelligence research, "divergent thinking" stands for the development of obvious, multiple logical conclusions from existing information (see Sect. 2.1), creativity can be defined as *thinking in different directions* and *searching for still open alternative possibilities*, whereby through the transfer or transformation of this information, e.g., due to analogy formation, new meanings are acquired (see Preiser, 1976, pp. 57 ff.).

To support these thoughts or mental actions, courage is also needed, namely "courage to leave gaps." Specifically, this means speculating freely whether the idea could work, or simply assuming or guessing, as recommended in creativity research ("making guesses," see Dow, 2022, p. 12).

3.2 Personality Traits Corresponding with Creativity

Creativity is not a "self-starter" and does not fill the "trait space" or the spectrum of traits as a characteristic or ability alone, but should always or often be seen and occur in connection with other psychological constructs or personality traits. For a later *differential diagnosis* of creativity (see Chap. 4), this fact, i.e., the collection and presentation of a trait profile, is important insofar as it offers the possibility to make plausibility considerations or tests in the assessment of creative performances or talents and to test the postulated relationship patterns.

That creativity is associated with intelligence as a general mental ability and prerequisite for creative achievements does not need further emphasis and repetition (see Chap. 2 and Sect. 3.1). Nevertheless, this connection should not be simply "blindly" adopted and accepted, as some limitations also appeared in earlier research results. Thus, it is a remarkable finding that an interaction between intelligence and creativity or a joint influence on school performance could *not* be established (see Preiser, 1976, p. 53). Highly creative schoolchildren are apparently less well-liked than highly intelligent students! Possibly, from the perspective of their teachers or educators, they are less well-adjusted children and not "easy to handle."

In line with this, creative people may be assumed to have a "drive-laden" and *regression tendency* in the psychoanalytic sense, which goes back to the subconscious. As a consequence, the sometimes expressed ideas and thoughts of "creative individuals" appeared childish and naive to other people and caused surprise or astonishment and possibly initially met with skepticism or rejection (cf. Preiser, 1976, pp. 67 ff.).

In order to make oneself heard and to assert oneself with these unusual ideas, the creative person very likely needs *self-confidence* or self-assurance and a certain degree of *willingness to take risks* – and, not to forget, a considerable amount of *self-motivation!* For creating, trying out, experimenting, and conducting explorations or investigations, *curiosity* is also needed as a driving force. *Tolerance of ambiguity* and conflict strength are likely to round off the personality profile of a creative individual, especially when "dry spells" or frustrating failures need to be overcome.

Dealing with contradictions seems to particularly distinguish creative individuals. Unlike others, they have *no* fear that their worldview of "right" or "wrong" will collapse, but they can handle "thesis" and "antithesis" well, as it is their endeavor to bring together and connect opposites on a higher level as "synthesis" (see Baudson, 2011).

Accompanying personality traits related to creativity can be found, as already mentioned, in various lists and compilations, among others, by Schuler and Görlich (2007) (see Sect. 3.1). From the literature, the following additions can be made, which are at least worth considering:

1. Creativity could depend on the "love" for a particular activity, as is often observed in the arts. A quote from Torrance (1988, p. 68) may clarify this requirement: *"Being in love with what one is doing"!*
2. The love for an activity is also related to *intrinsic* motivation. It is responsible for creative achievements, along with self-determination and the perseverance to repeatedly and continuously engage with and be enthusiastic about a particular activity (see Hennessey & Amaible, 1988, p. 13).
3. More of a cognitive challenge is the already mentioned problem sensitivity, which here concretizes in the requirement to redefine problems or tasks combined with the generation of hypotheses as an additional facet of creativity, as Torrance (1988, pp. 46 f.) postulated.

Not to be forgotten, in the creation of creations, an own will, or a "liberal spirit," as Tardif and Sternberg (1988, pp. 433 ff.) demanded, is necessary, and the detachment from a *"conventional limitation"* (see e.g., Wienkamp, 2022a, p. 28), which stands in the way of new unusual thoughts or ideas or unorthodox thinking.

With the exception of the already cited studies by Schuler and Görlich (2007, pp. 12 f. and 69) based on the *"16-PF personality test"* by Cattel and colleagues, no correlative relationships between creativity and other personality traits had been known and quantified up to that point.

Hennessey and Amaible (1988, pp. 32 ff.) also pointed out some studies on the influence of *self-confidence ("self-esteem")* on creativity. For example, in different environmental conditions in the experiment (i.e., in the experimental group with observation and assessment of behavior, in the control group without), shy or timid subjects showed less creativity in the tasks given (e.g., writing a fantasy story) than when they were not under observation (with assessment). Subjects with a high level of self-confidence showed comparable creativity performances both under observation and in the control group, which were above the level of subjects with low self-confidence. Besides self-confidence, a well-developed *resilience,* defined as "mental resilience," may also have contributed. Strength and power as an expression of a strong will, combined with sufficient own resources, serve self-regulation (and self-efficacy) in dealing with stressful, challenging situations (see e.g., Kuhl, 2010, p. 377).

In a negative sense, with regard to "creativity barriers," it should be mentioned that complex and negatively noticeable thoughts or "sets," such as *"functional fixedness"* as the inability to see an object differently than before, were also relevant for creativity research. The same applies to *rigidity* as the inability to overcome or dismantle once acquired mental schemas (see Seiffge-Krenke, 1974, p. 101).

3.3 Creativity as a Process

Following the discussion about personality traits in connection with creativity or creative achievements as an observable product, the creativity process has recently also sparked interest in creativity research in general and in creativity diagnostics in particular. Creativity could thus unfold or result in the form of a process over various stages or sequences. Along the defined process stages, different requirements are posed to creativity as a construct and the personality traits as well as cognitive abilities such as intelligence that interact with it, which on the one hand should be examined separately for each phase and on the other hand should be operationalized in a multimodal approach or design.

The creativity process can be organized and structured according to the prevailing opinion in the literature as per Table 3.1.

Against the background of this process or phase model of creativity, the sequences inevitably belong together and define creativity based on the observable achievements and behavior. However, it is also clear that the focus or center of creative processes lies in the conception phase, as this is where new ideas (as a creative achievement or product) arise through different mental activities. Other models in the literature also predominantly follow a "four-phase model," but refer to the clarification phase mentioned here as the *Incubation Phase* and the conception phase as the *Illumination Phase*. An operationalization of the activities or facets belonging to creativity would fundamentally be possible through "thinking aloud" by the subjects, including observation and documentation, if psychometric methods such as a creativity test do not help further.

3.4 Creativity and Innovation Capability

Creativity fundamentally precedes innovation as the actual implementation process; it is therefore the crucial prerequisite or trigger for new innovative products and services. Creativity in the field of business and technology is closely linked to corporate knowledge management, which contains resources or sources in the

Table 3.1 The Creative Process

No.	Phase	Creative Achievements and Behavior	Focus
1	Initial Phase	1) Problem Perception (Sensitivity) 2) Problem Identification (Recognition)	= > Infection
2	Clarification Phase	1) Recall or Reactivation of "Old or Prior Knowledge" 2) Redefinition of the Problem or Reorganization of Knowledge (Asking Questions) 3) Information Search and Selection	= > Deepening
3	Conception Phase	1) Imaginations (Fantasies, Mental Images) 2) Development of Alternatives (Hypotheses) (Perspective Change, Combinations) 3) Idea Generation	= > Creation
4	Verification Phase	1) Filtering and Selection 2) Testing and if necessary Feedback (Loop Formation) 3) Calculations and Evaluation	= > Validation

form of knowledge and makes them available for creations that are then developed and created by "human hands."

If an organization, such as a company, wants to maintain the ability to solve problems of any kind (e.g., inventions or patents), it cannot do without creative employees who know, perceive, and also detect or pursue the problems on-site at their workplaces or at the "customer front." However, these employees at the grassroots level rarely come into the world as "geniuses" or bring creativity that helps the company and advances it, not so easily after their vocational training or studies. After starting their careers, new employees must first be developed into experts or specialists in their field through both *training on the job* and *training off the job*. Therefore, personnel development as a corporate function must keep creativity or problem-solving ability in view as a crucial and most important corporate requirement and promote these requirement characteristics through appropriate measures in the entrepreneurial sense.

Some authors (see, for example, the anthology by Landes et al., 2022) therefore hold the view that a distinction should be made between creativity and innovations, as innovation usually follows the "creative creation" or the new idea. However, it is completely incomprehensible in this context that although "long lists" of personality traits exist in the specialist literature that aim to describe or characterize a creative personality, their trait relationships, admittedly judged controversially with pros and cons scientifically, did not include the indication in the relevant contributions that, given the difficulties in measuring creativity (see Chap. 4), research on the "creative personality" largely still moves at the level of postulates or speculations and that findings published in the meantime should always be taken with caution and only have a provisional statement value!

Genius inventors are not necessarily to be expected "across the board," as most company members do not enter and work in the research and development areas (R&D areas) as researchers or designers. But especially in production or marketing, in contact with the customer, new challenges are to be expected and mastered daily, which require noticeable problem-solving competence. Progressive organizations therefore rely on professional innovation management, which enjoys and possesses the blessing of the company management or the board.

The core of innovation management is to collect the many mostly rather randomly occurring or arisen ideas at the workplaces and convert them into usable innovations, e.g., initially as prototypes and later as new products. Innovation or knowledge management naturally also includes ideas or inventions that are not immediately usable, so it is advisable, for example, to archive these ideas in a designated "expert system" and have access to them at any time through an appropriate system (e.g., a keyword register or similar). For this type of "idea or innovation management," completely different human requirements are demanded and required than in the R&D lab for "genius inventors." A professional innovation management is certainly not to be compared with the "venerable" and now outdated "company suggestion scheme (in German: BVW)" as a central institution e.g. in German companies (see Wienkamp, 2023a, p. 93 f.).

For *innovators*, it mainly comes down to *leadership* and *management skills* if they want to successfully "carry through" their projects. They must constantly convince others of the necessity of their actions and bring them to their side. Without a high degree of assertiveness and influence in the sense of *"tactical skill"*, this is not feasible. As project or product managers, they are also responsible for the planning, organization, and control of their tasks, which distinguishes them as managers. For example, they have to develop a new drug or a cosmetic as a product innovation from a new active ingredient created by research and "bring it to the man or woman."

If a "strategic innovation management" is established as an institution in the company, this institution has the constant task of reviewing the many creations or ideas and regularly checking them for realization opportunities. This includes, in addition to technical feasibility, the examination of market attractiveness as well as the calculation of the necessary expenses and resources. Of the human requirements for innovation management already mentioned and listed elsewhere (see Wienkamp, 2021a, p. 244), the *"intuition"* is particularly noteworthy, which reveals itself in a sensitivity to so-called *weak signals,* whether inconsistencies or a still hidden ("dormant") customer need, for which new previously unimagined applications or product solutions are offered, whose necessary basic technologies, however, were primarily created by other "inventors" in basic research.

3.5 Summary

Creativity has become a "buzzword" as a requirement characteristic. Most authors agree with this assessment in their publications or contributions. At the same time, they hold the opinion that creativity is indispensable "as a driver" or source of innovations or new products. The "research community" is not in agreement about what exactly creativity is and how it relates to or distinguishes itself from intelligence.

Thus, it was necessary in this contribution to name and highlight the main criteria for creations such as new ideas or inventions, namely originality, usefulness, and social acceptance both within an organization and later in the market towards potential customers. Nevertheless, it seems undisputed that creative achievements do not arise from nothing but necessarily rely on experiential knowledge as a basis, and the creative idea generators have usually repeatedly engaged with the problem to be solved. Often, these creative people, such as artists, develop a genuine passion or love for their occupation—and become better or more creative over time.

Creativity does not appear in isolation but is flanked, accompanied, and supported by other personality traits. For example, a certain willingness to take risks, along with the necessary self-confidence, can be identified in creative individuals to engage with the idea repeatedly and to make themselves heard by others. That creative people are naturally more curious and possess a good basic intelligence probably goes without saying.

Creative achievements do not arise suddenly but usually follow a timeline that goes through certain sequences. For this reason, it is unavoidable to take a closer look at the creativity process from the perception of an open problem to the problem-solving through a creative proposal, especially with regard to creativity diagnostics.

However, the ability to innovate is associated with entirely different ideas of skills and personality dispositions. Innovators are less the inventors but *pragmatic* thinking and acting managers who implement the ideas conceived by others into innovative product solutions and are responsible for the development or innovation process up to market launch.

Attempts at Creativity Diagnostics

4

In addressing the topic of creativity diagnostics, the aim is not to redefine or describe what creativity is (as in Chap. 3), but rather to address and discuss the specific problem situations of any form of diagnostics or assessment of creative achievements. It cannot be ruled out that creativity diagnostics in an ordinary form may not exist or cannot exist because creative behavior does not manifest or unfold "in orderly paths" and therefore cannot be assessed unequivocally and directly. The specific problems of creativity diagnostics are as follows:

1. Firstly, in the problem itself, since "open problems" cannot easily be operationalized and prescribed from the outside (or by other persons, such as in a candidate selection process).
2. Even if a suitable problem is found, the so-called "incubation period" leads to the impossibility for the affected individuals to respond promptly or within a certain time. During the incubation period, an indeterminate "fermentation process" occurs until a possible solution is reached, which mostly takes place in the subconscious and unexpectedly or unpredictably manifests as a spontaneous idea.
3. Ideas or spontaneous expressions of thought are often still very unrefined, and their occurrence appears impulsive, which affects the evaluation of ideas or their qualitative assessment. Misunderstandings, misinterpretations, or knowledge gaps of the evaluators cannot be ruled out in such situations. Moreover, it is only in exceptional cases that evaluators can prepare themselves with appropriate evaluation criteria for spontaneously expressed ideas. The most suitable evaluation criteria are the number and type of questions that the subject either poses to themselves or directs, or how they redefine the task in front of the audience to find a solution approach.
4. Furthermore, creativity is not the same as (or not always) problem-solving ability, which often follows rational-logical steps or considerations. Creativity can sometimes initially lead to chaos in thinking until a "solution sketch" (or figure) emerges. There is certainly no single true or correct solution when dealing with creativity (see Sect. 3.1).

H. Wienkamp, *Creativity Diagnostics*, https://doi.org/10.1007/978-3-662-70432-5_4

5. It is questionable whether the previously known methods, such as creativity tests, can tackle the problem of creativity diagnostics. If creativity tests measure problem-solving ability, they are not actually creativity tests but rather cognitive performance tests or apparent intelligence tests, which generally only recognize and allow right or wrong answers or solutions.

Attempts at creativity diagnostics have been made using both standardized psychometric and projective methods.

Projective test methods, such as the *"Thematic Apperception Test (TAT)"* by Murray (1938) or the well-known *Rorschach Test* with its "inkblots" as picture cards, were used in modified form mainly in the educational diagnostics of schoolchildren as a "fantasy test".

In adults, projective methods were also used in earlier studies that attempted to determine a "disposition for originality" or mental complexity (see e.g., Barron, 1965, pp. 39 ff.). In all studies, the evaluators faced a dilemma in deciding whether the test subject's responses were original or not. Barron (1965, pp. 15 ff.) commented on this as follows: *"The Rorschach scorer was certain that the subject's responses were 'originals,' for the test manual defines an original response as one that occurs no more often than once in 100 examinations; but whether to score the responses 0 + [a 'good' original] or 0—[an original response that does not sufficiently respect the inkblot reality] was difficult to decide."*

Tendentially, members of the "original group" defined here seem to master both impulse control and regression tendency, allowing them to behave both childishly naive and strictly rational (see e.g., the findings cited by Seiffge-Krenke, 1974, pp. 62 ff.). Regardless of these results pointing in a certain direction, suggesting that there are apparently connections between cognitive complexity and creativity, the investigative methods used, such as projective tests, are very questionable and subject to criticism in their psychometric criteria.

The construction of diagnostic methods such as creativity tests should also be based on cognitive performances, whether they are metacognitions or transfer performances. Specific tasks or items should be assigned to or derived from these cognitions through prior hypothesis formation and developed accordingly. After experimental verification, the cognitive abilities or factors should be extracted and identified from the results using statistical methods (e.g., factor analysis). For the subjects, the investigations focus on recognizing *hidden* connections, similarities, or analogies, as well as the occurrence of *critical* events such as narrow pass or "bottlenecks." Additionally, there are requirements that induce a *subjective* experience such as insights, intuition, inspiration, etc.

In general, these cognitive performances or abilities are used within a process chain that began with problem recognition and ended with the evaluation or assessment of the idea. Without a sensitivity to problems and an intuition for inconsistencies, hidden, non-obvious problems do not become apparent at all. On the other hand, fantasies or the mental imagination of possible consequences or development paths, cognitive restructuring such as flexibility, perspective change or redefinition of tasks, dealing with complexity or multivariate events, and last but not least, the courage to develop ideas are the qualities without which creative demands could not be met.

Many cognitive demands have been elevated and introduced as standard in business practice, either as requirement characteristics through a *psychological requirements analysis* (see Wienkamp, 2020b, 2021a, b, 2022c) or as assessment characteristics in business evaluation systems (see Wienkamp, 2022b), such as the characteristic *complexity management* as potential for leadership and management functions. But also "curiosity" as another potential characteristic should not be missing in a discussion about creativity and should find its rightful place (see, for example, the requirement profile of a personnel manager with success-critical, i.e., positive and negative behaviors in Wienkamp, 2023a, pp. 10 f.).

4.1 Creativity Tests

Creativity tests are or were increasingly used in the examination or assessment of preschool and school children. Research with this age cohort has set significant accents for further creativity diagnostics, also in the construction of creativity tests, which began with preschool and school children and on which test developments for older age groups were oriented.

In occupational aptitude diagnostics, creativity tests can also be used, which were specifically developed for this application purpose. Some test instruments adopted the experiences gained from the school sector.

Both in the creativity diagnostics of children and adults, there are still many unresolved problems, which are primarily due to the peculiarities of this characteristic creativity.

4.1.1 Creativity Tests in Educational Diagnostics

Already in early childhood, such as in preschool age, efforts began to prove creative talents or abilities in children. Without wanting to go into the individual observations or research results in detail, it remains to be noted that creativity diagnostics was more an investigation of the *"social milieu"* or social origin, as the social status of the family and the parenting style of the home, such as the habit of openly discussing problems, were decisive for the child's creative performances.

In later school age, creative students, according to the observations of teachers and test results, especially when using the *"Torrance Test,"* were simply "more broadly positioned" if they could simultaneously be enthusiastic about "Shakespeare and dolls" (Seiffge-Krenke, 1974, p. 135).

In, for example, a *"Toy-Improvement Test"* with three toys (one more for boys, one for girls, and one neutral), creative children were able to be more interested in all toys and came up with more uses than non-creative children, who only befriended the gender-typical toy and primarily played with it.

One of the most comprehensive contributions to creativity diagnostics in the German-speaking area was the already frequently cited contribution by Seiffge-Krenke (1974). At that time, Seiffge-Krenke not only summarized the results of creativity research but also conducted an empirical study on school children in the 4th grade at an average age of 10 years. She pursued three questions in her work, which are still of interest in creativity diagnostics today:

1) The influence of instructions either with or without time constraints (which is also associated with stress)
2) The assessment of the creativity of a target person by both teachers and classmates
3) Psychometric investigation of the validity of creativity tasks used in tests

As a creativity test, the *Torrance Test* in German translation and in adapted form (see Seiffge-Krenke, 1974, in the appendix p. 289 ff.) was used with the creativity characteristics

a) Fluency: The number of ideas or suggestions mentioned was measured or counted (e.g., the possible uses for a tin can);
b) Flexibility: The "breadth" or spectrum of the expressed ideas was measured or recorded, i.e., how many different categories, predetermined by a list, the mentioned ideas fell into;
c) Originality: Originality was determined based on the frequency or rarity of the expected responses in a sample population according to a predetermined grid;
d) Elaboration: Elaborations, when identified as such in individual cases, received an additional bonus point for indicating unusual ideas or detailed and highlighted details that stood out as "embellishments".

In the creativity study, stress-inducing instructions negatively affected creativity performance, as if the participants (in this case, schoolchildren) could complete the given creativity tasks more playfully without time constraints. This finding was also expected in this form.

The different instructional conditions were evaluated using a variance analytical procedure and tested for statistically significant mean differences in the creativity characteristics. As expected, pupils achieved the best results under the condition "no time limitation" and "abstention from additional stress induction". Under this condition, the pupils could approach the creativity test playfully and in their own way, almost relaxed. *Fluency,* meaning many ideas or suggestions, and *originality* were the creativity characteristics that best differentiated with their mean values between the different instructions.

Pupils and teachers did not differ in their judgments of what creativity is or who in the respective class was considered creative (named) and who, in contrast, was not creative (also named). The "creative" (or the "non-creative" with low ratings) could be statistically correctly assigned by both survey groups using the total values of the creativity characteristics (plus intelligence as a second variable) when applying a discriminant analysis. The assessment procedure of teachers and pupils corresponded to an extreme group comparison, whereby the teachers named only five pupils of a class as "creative" and also five schoolchildren as "non-creative", while the pupils assessed all classmates of the class, including themselves, regarding creativity.

As a control variable, the personal style of the class teacher was recorded among the students in terms of emotional support and the extent of control towards the schoolchildren. The pedagogical approach or the "teacher style" did not have a significant influence on the pupils' assessments.

Correlation analyses of the creativity attributes showed in the psychometric examination and assessment that the same characteristics from different subtests correlated significantly lower than the different creativity characteristics within a subtest with each other. Such findings contradict construct validity and strongly indicate a "material factor" (see Seiffge-Krenke, 1974, p. 254) when creativity performance mainly depends on the task or the test used.

Bollinger (1981) agreed with these findings on creativity measurement insofar as he concluded, after evaluating a multitude of studies with various tests on "divergent thinking", which were primarily used in the school sector for creativity diagnostics, that these tests, despite demonstrable correlations to intelligence, capture divergent thinking but are not suitable for measuring creativity. Decisive for this assessment were, on the one hand, contradictory factor structures and incomparable test implementations when the tests were conducted, for example, *with* or *without* standardized time constraints. Further uncertainties arose both in the definition of creative performances or products and in the selection and handling of assessment criteria, making comparability between the studies on creativity as output hardly possible.

Krampen et al. (1990) did not assess the state of creativity diagnostics in preschool and school children quite as negatively. For the age groups 4–12 years, they compiled a test battery as a developmental psychology test called *"Creativity Test for Preschool and School Children (KVS)"*, whose 7 subtests were based on already existing test procedures. All test tasks had in common that they could be applied without language comprehension and focused on "kinesthetic and figural-pictorial divergent abilities," as the test authors expressed it. There were *no* time constraints for the test tasks and no other instructions that exerted pressure on the children; on the contrary, the subtests were to be completed in a playful and absolutely "relaxed" manner. Two observers created test protocols, which were evaluated as external assessments according to the criteria

1) Idea fluency or productivity,
2) Originality (for rare or unexpected solutions),
3) Flexibility,
4) Elaboration,
5) Imaginations

on a five-point scale. This made it possible to determine both the interrater reliability between the observers and the validity with parallel assessments by parents and teachers (also as external assessments) regarding the children's creativity according to the aforementioned criteria outside the test situation. The authors were generally satisfied with the quality criteria of this KVS, although the factor structure with only *four* main components as confirmation of the creativity performances according to the aforementioned five assessment criteria did not meet expectations.

In a later contribution, Urban (2011) compiled the creativity tests published in the German-speaking area for educational diagnostics in the school sector. This list also included the *"Test for Creative Thinking—Drawing (TSD—Z)"* constructed by Urban and Jellen (1995; cited in Urban, 2011) for children aged 4 to 16 years.

4.1.2 Creativity Tests in Vocational Aptitude Diagnostics

Among the early attempts to diagnose creativity in adults, the *"Brick-Uses Test"* is certainly one of the most well-known tests. The task was to find as many uses for a brick as possible within a given time frame. Instead of a brick, other objects could also be conceivable and selectable (such as tin cans, see Sect. 4.1.1). This principle as a task was later adopted in other creativity tests, and the number of ideas presented was used as a measure or criterion of creativity. Various evaluators can assess the quality of the ideas based on an evaluation scheme, from which the interrater agreement can then be calculated as reliability.

In all these standardized creativity tests, such as the "Torrance Test," on the one hand, the time restriction seems to contradict the measurement of creativity (see already Sect. 4.1.1), and on the other hand, they do not address the fact that creativity cannot be summoned on demand and is not temporally stable, but, as noted by some researchers, follows a temporal rhythm (see Guilford, 1950 and already Chap. 3).

A number of authors have repeatedly expressed criticism regarding the aspect of validity. For example, mentioning many uses for a brick says nothing about creativity in everyday life situations, as Seiffge-Krenke (1974, p. 181) emphasized. Due to potential assessment errors in external ratings, teacher assessments, for example, are also controversial as evidence of criterion validity when it comes to current and especially prospective assessments, such as a child's suitability for a particular educational path.

Assessments by managers as superiors seem to be more suitable, as managers experience both the performance and behavior of their employees daily and over a longer period and must also recognize and accept "creative performances" as such. Certainly, a positive vote is only to be expected if the new idea is useful and corresponds to reality. When managers assess creativity, it does not necessarily mean that they rely on identical or uniform criteria, as they belong to different business areas or disciplines, each with their own ideas of creativity in their field, and they may also have individually different preferences regarding the personal or general significance of creativity.

Thus, the circle closes on the topic of creativity as an essentially indefinable, tangible, and therefore not reliably measurable phenomenon in creativity diagnostics. Creativity as a multiple construct creates for many personnel managers a not necessarily compatible or comparable image of the target person, and anyone who tries to assess creativity must communicate their definition or idea of it, such as in an aptitude diagnostic examination. A definition of creativity could consist of it being primarily an imaginative performance (imagination), that is, a thought process enriched with "sparkling imagination," whose idea or content must then be evaluated or "tapped" by a "jury" for its usefulness, sense of reality, etc. Both, namely novelty and usefulness, as mentioned elsewhere, would then be the decisive evaluation criteria of creativity for an assessment group. Something unique or non-repeatable, which expresses genius, however, is unlikely to meet expectations and reality and certainly does not help in everyday situations. Nevertheless, admittedly, there are quite limited possibilities in the approach to discover artistic-aesthetic talents. However, this would presuppose operationalizing and determining such a special talent, for example, through tasks with design requirements (see the exemplary tasks A and B in Appendix 1).

It almost borders on a miracle that there have nevertheless been attempts in recent years to develop creativity tests. Already in another publication (see Wienkamp, 2021a, p. 184 ff.), two different creativity tests were mentioned as examples that have appeared in recent years and are supposed to be specifically suitable for occupational aptitude diagnostics. One was the *"Creativity Test for Technical-Scientific Professions"* by Facaoaru (1985), and the other was the test for *"Diagnostics of Job-Related Creativity for Technical and Developmental Activities (DBK-TE)"* by Palmer (2016) for the technical-industrial sector. Facaoaru's instrument was very much based on the model of divergent and convergent thinking propagated by Guilford at the time (see also Schuler & Görlich, 2007, p. 20 f.), while Palmer's test attempts to simulate the creativity process and measure the creativity observed in the process.

4.1.2.1 The Creativity Test by Facaoaru (1985)

In the item selection, Facaoaru's test further differentiated between tasks with a subject-specific vs. general problem statement and tasks with only one correct solution (as in an intelligence test) and multiple possible solutions, as is typical for creative tasks. The focus or goal of this test was to find a synthesis between divergent and convergent thinking and to design corresponding problem statements as test tasks.

For this purpose, Facaoaru developed subtests, namely, on the one hand, to formulate complete sentences from incomplete word combinations on a suitable topic, and on the other hand, to recognize and draw a complete picture or scenario from line drawings or also incomplete sketches, or to "embellish" the line drawings. This test was validated on researchers in science and engineers in construction. As a result, it was shown, as expected, that these two professional groups pursue different *work styles*. While scientists proceed analytically and hypothesis-driven, engineers are more concerned with a quick and global solution to their technical problem.

Whether this comparison of work styles can also make a statement about creativity and its manifestations or qualities in these professions remains to be seen.

4.1.2.2 The "DBK-TE" by Palmer (2016)

The "DBK-TE" by Palmer (2016) followed the process model of Schuler and Görlich (2007). Problems or test tasks were oriented towards possible solutions for a given technical problem, and the evaluation was based on the number of proposals presented for the individual process steps from problem perception to the implementation of the problem solution, thus corresponding to an "open response format." Relevant expertise as prior knowledge was, of course, not required for completing the tasks. For example, it may concern whether the test person recognizes the problem at all, which missing information they would need to seek, which solution concepts (e.g., forming analogies) they possess, etc. Only independent and meaningful answers received a point when processing the test tasks, while redundant or nonsensical answers were not considered.

Overall, this "DBK-TE" consists of *15 test tasks,* including two simulations and 13 tasks with open problems. Evaluations or result interpretations are possible both at the level of the test tasks and at the level of the *eight* stages or process steps. With one exception, each process stage contains two test tasks that characterize this sequence and are typical for it according to the requirements.

The development of the test tasks (items) was preceded by a requirements analysis based on the *"Critical Incident Technique (CIT)"* by Flanagan (1954) at various companies. Based on this data, different test versions could be tested and selected until the final version, with, as already mentioned, 13 verbally answered tasks and additionally two simulation tasks. The selection among the test tasks was made both according to the usual psychometric quality criteria and by an "expert panel" based on the content consistency and representativeness of creativity in the workplace or practice (i.e., face validity). For example, a verbally answered task was to "find a secure holder for the ignition key for a ride-on lawnmower (so that it does not fall out and get lost)," and as a simulation task, for example, (according to the instruction) good arguments should be found for a "board presentation" to preferentially present one's own project over a competitor pursuing the same goal or intention. In the two simulation tasks, observers also evaluated only self-developed and presented arguments, e.g., during a role play or a presentation.

For validation, the subjects were supposed to provide various self-assessments regarding their creativity, career success, job satisfaction, etc., in addition to completing intelligence tests and selected personality tests, which, however, as self-assessments, were largely not effective and successful in attempting to validate the test. The author herself lamented the lack of a suitable and objective *external criterion,* e.g., considering a supervisor's assessment as an external evaluation and validity criterion alongside the level of salary or other bonuses or incentives for creative achievements.

Evaluations and interpretations of the test results are possible and meaningful both on the basis of the tasks and at the process level. Since the test encompasses and runs through all phases of a "creative process" to the end, it poses demands on creativity on the one hand, and on the *innovative capacity* in the implementation or realization of the problem solution on the other. However, in a later model analysis, the existence of both creativity and innovation as latent constructs could (still) not be demonstrated according to the available empirical data, which is not surprising (see Sect. 3.4). In contrast, in thinking, the model analysis suggested a *two-factor structure* of "divergent thinking" on the one hand and "evaluative thinking" on the other, alongside a one-factor solution (see Palmer, 2016, p. 239 f.).

The complete view of the events or the course of a creativity process is an advantage on the one hand, but can also become a disadvantage on the other if the different demands on "creative inventors" and "innovators" as project managers are disregarded and lead to false conclusions. A way out would be, simultaneously with the creativity test, to also assess *management qualities* through personality tests with the corresponding leadership and management requirements, alongside general intelligence, curiosity (or "openness to new experiences"), and achievement motivation as probable predictors or influencing factors for creativity (see also Sect. 4.3 and Chap. 7).

In addition to these creativity tests, the *"Berlin Intelligence Structure Test (BIS–4)"* by Jäger et al. (1997) with the creativity-measuring feature scale *"Ingenuity"* and the creativity test by Schuler et al. (2013), the *"DBK-PG"* (see Sect. 4.1.2.4), which was the first creativity test to follow a process model, should also be mentioned.

4.1.2.3 The Feature Scale "Ingenuity" in the "BIS-4" by Jäger et al. (1997)

Unlike the creativity tests presented so far, the already mentioned "BIS-4" by Jäger et al. (1997) is not a creativity test, but an intelligence test with a feature scale that aims to capture creative performance as an intelligence component, namely "ingenuity." Ingenuity is defined as the production of many new and diverse ideas. Behind such specific test requirements lie, according to the jargon, "idea fluency" as the quantity of creative ideas or concepts and "idea flexibility" as the diversity in the use of different categories or qualities in application.

According to the structure of the "BIS-4," the feature ingenuity (abbr. E) includes a total of *12 tasks,* which appear in *figural-pictorial, verbal,* and *numerical forms.* For example, according to the task description of the test (see Jäger et al., 1997, p. 68 ff.), the following operationalizations are provided for this feature:

1) Scale Layout (LO) as a figural-pictorial form
   = "As many different graphic emblems (identification marks) as possible should be designed for an advertisement of a small store";
2) Scale Insight Test (IT) as a verbal form

= "For a verbally given situation, as many different explanations as possible should be provided";

3) Scale Phone Numbers (TN) as a numerical form
= "The task is to construct as many x-digit phone numbers as possible, which should be structured so regularly that they are easy to memorize; the rules used should be as varied as possible".

This "BIS-4" test is to be applied for intelligence measurement among pupils or students of all school types and age groups. Since intelligence tests are often used for the selection of trainees in companies, for example, to validate school grades, the BIS-4 also falls into the category of vocational aptitude tests. Norms as standard values for interindividual comparison are available for the age groups. A specific variant is the "BIS-HB" as an intelligence test for normally and highly gifted pupils with a norming for the age groups from 12 to 16 years (see e.g., Frenzel & Nett, 2008; https://www.researchgate.net/publication/352264865).

All responses of the test subjects to the "E-tasks" are to be recorded and evaluated by at least *two test administrators* according to the already mentioned criteria of idea fluency as a quantitative measure and idea diversity as a qualitative measure, measured by the categories produced by the client. Corresponding protocol sheets and a manual with instructions and application examples are available to support the test administrators. Specifically for this feature ingenuity/idea flexibility, the test manual contains a list of categories with corresponding examples, which the test administrators can use as a guide during evaluation. After evaluation, a "raw score" is available for each intelligence performance and text form, which is to be converted into "standard values" using age norms.

As a test result, individual results are available for all 12 test tasks of the feature ingenuity, which are to be aggregated and prepared as "task bundles" for the three different test forms. All results of the intelligence test are included in the calculation to determine the overall score as "general intelligence." Incidentally, the feature ingenuity correlated with the overall test score "general intelligence" (or also the IQ) with $r = 0.70$.

The unity of divergent and convergent thinking as "essential components" of problem-solving ability, which the intelligence model of Jäger et al. (1997) was based on (cf. König, 1986), speaks in favor of a joint creativity and intelligence diagnostics. Proponents of integrating creativity and intelligence as intellectual abilities within the framework of intelligence diagnostics nevertheless conceded that very different abilities and mental operations are hidden behind these intellectual qualities, which argue against a summary "under a common roof (of intelligence)." Not without reason, intelligence research and diagnostics have long given preference to convergent thinking for various obvious reasons and have treated divergent thinking "stepmotherly," that is, neglected it. If creativity diagnostics is limited to the assessment of fluid (i.e., the number of ideas), flexible (i.e., the diversity of ideas), and original ideas as an expression of the "unusual" or rare, it can be assumed with limitations that there is an *independent* creativity factor as a personality trait, which stands out from the other intellectual performances of intelligence diagnostics.

In the validation studies of the "Berlin Intelligence Structure Test," intellectual abilities loaded divergent and convergent thinking together with other personality traits such as motivation, interests, and self-concept highly on a *common* general factor. This means that divergent and convergent thinking is a complex construct of general intellectual performance capacity, which, together with other personality dispositions, conditions and creates the prerequisites for problem-solving abilities in various situations and with different challenges (cf. König, 1986).

4.1.2.4 The "DBK-PG" by Schuler et al. (2013)

Before the DBK-TE by Palmer (2016), Schuler et al. (2013) developed a creativity test for the first time, called *"Diagnosis of Job-Related Creativity—Planning and Design (DBK-PG)"* based on a process design conceived by Schuler and Görlich (2007). This creativity test was intended particularly for vocational aptitude diagnostics or for personnel selection as well as for career counseling or similar purposes. Similar to the already introduced DBK-TE, this test contains, as a process model of creativity, the already mentioned eight process stages, namely from problem discovery to the implementation of the problem solution. The theoretical idea associated with breaking down creativity into phases or process stages was that test subjects could indeed bring in and display different facets of creativity or their personality during the process steps, which, due to changing demands on creativity, could even manifest as task-specific strengths or weaknesses (see the test review by Pundt, 2014).

To make it easier for test takers and thus also to support the "social validity" or acceptance of a test application, the test constructors embedded the creativity test in a "cover story" as *"Establishment or Redesign of a City Park."* For the eight sequences of creativity tasks to be completed, the test subjects were to generate or name as many ideas, peculiarities (problems), or arguments as possible. The number of free responses provided a measure or indicator of their "idea fluency." A separate evaluation of other creativity indicators, such as flexibility and originality, was deliberately omitted due to the high intercorrelations with idea fluency.

For example, the test subjects were to:

- Identify and name problems in a newspaper article,
- Combine possible uses of objects (e.g., fallen fruit or branches) for a possible game (e.g., baseball),
- Develop arguments either against the establishment or redesign of the city park altogether or counter criticism of individual measures.

Meaningful and non-replicated mentions received one or, depending on the task variant, several points, resulting in a certain point total that was to be converted into standard scores or norms as a "raw score." For the sole factor "creativity" as a construct, the evaluation scheme was as follows:

a) below-average creative abilities = $\leq$ 90 standard scores;

b) average creative abilities = 100 standard scores;
c) above-average creative abilities = ≥ 110 standard scores.

Since the test as a whole test across all process phases achieved better psychometric properties than in the individual process sections, the instrument unfortunately failed to achieve an important goal, namely to generate a phase-dependent creativity profile, as the test developers probably imagined, expected, and perhaps wished for, which closely aligns with the respective creativity requirements (see also Pundt, 2014).

4.2 Other Methods for Creativity Diagnostics

Open questions about an everyday problem in job interviews are popular as a method for checking or diagnosing creative responses. The HR representative as the interviewer can adequately prepare for this and compare a considerable number of possible answers with the statements or arguments presented by the applicant. Under certain circumstances, the applicant may express very creative solutions that the HR representative or their company has not yet considered! However, such an event is of a highly rare nature and additionally requires a "reality check." More likely, the interviewer will find a series of the applicant's mentions on his or her list.

Open problem questions for an applicant interview could be, for example:

a) You are facing a technical problem (e.g., opening a can) and do not have the appropriate tool at hand (e.g., no can opener). What alternatives could you possibly resort to?
b) A client presentation is scheduled for today at noon as part of a contract bid. At 9:00, the designated client advisor or project manager calls you to say that they cannot conduct the client presentation as planned because they have just had a car accident and must seek medical treatment for at least today. What would you do?

Unfortunately, it is the case that such interview questions often address or diagnose something other than creativity or the like. Just as well, one could think of, for example, resilience, stress resistance, or responsiveness as so-called quick-wittedness in tense situations with surprise maneuvers (i.e., the "coping" of stress-inducing situations), as is the case in a job interview. In addition to dealing with stress, self-confidence or self-assurance usually accompany as personality traits, which, as already indicated, are positively related to creativity.

In emergency situations, as highlighted in question b), it is likely not only about creativity but also, or especially, about management skills such as planning and organization to master this critical situation.

Regardless of the question of the right and situation-appropriate personality traits, HR experts need evaluation schemes or a "manageable grid" to assess the applicants' reactions or statements. Simply recording the interviewees' answers is too cumbersome and only partially suitable for judgment, even if the recording is limited to keywords or short comments. Against the background of the evaluation grids already recommended in the literature (see, e.g., Fyock, 2008; Wienkamp, 2021a, p. 191), the schema presented in Table 4.1 could help in assessing creativity.

Five additional different problem cases for aptitude diagnostic examinations, which could be considered with the proposed evaluation system for creativity diagnostics, are, as already indicated, found in Appendix 1. The proposed problem cases involve both *artistic-aesthetic challenges* and problem cases from the *social milieu* involving other people. The former involves tasks such as designing a garden or furnishing an apartment. Here, the focus is on creative achievements in design and embellishment to create something "beautiful." The three social problem situations involve "conflicts" within the family regarding the settlement of an inheritance matter, as well as interpersonal problems in the workplace, e.g., in competence disputes due to interface problems in the work process or regarding responsibility and accountability for customer relationships. Additionally, both prudent and "creative" actions are required in an accident involving multiple people, whether it involves initiating an emergency call or providing "first aid."

A stronger connection to problem-solving ability in terms of analytics and creativity is certainly offered by *case studies,* as they are typically applied parallel to applicant interviews or, for example, preferably used in the context of training for "Management Business Administration," i.e., MBA education. With the case presentation and the comprehensive information on the matter provided as "supplementary material," the aim is particularly to stimulate imagination, such as what needs to be undertaken in the context of problem analysis, which additional information and insights are important, and how the abundance of details can be

Table 4.1 Evaluation scheme for assessing reactions to "open" problems

No.	Reaction or Statement	Evaluation	
		symbolic	verbal
1	Does not understand the task or problem	**(– –)**	**Very negative**
2	Merely repeats the facts or instructions or only states platitudes (does not get to the point and does not progress)	**(–)**	**Negative**
3	Redefines the task and seeks (in vain?) a reference or connection point (probes)	**0**	**Neutral**
4	Links the task with previous experiences or knowledge and interprets the task based on their own opinion or standpoint (reflects)	**(+)**	**Positive**
5	Additionally asks specific questions or formulates conditions for a possible solution path (sets the direction)	**(+ +)**	**Very positive**
6	Either spontaneously or after some consideration, finds a concrete solution or has a good (original) idea and is convinced of it themselves (shows initial creativity)	**(+ + +)**	**Excellent**

bundled and synthesized into a coherent concept and solution path. From applied business administration or management consulting, there is an overwhelming number of cases that these cover stories can draw upon. For example, there are:

a) Corporate takeovers (Mergers & Acquisitions or M&A transactions), which must be conducted either from the function of the *merger*, i.e., the buyer of the target company as the target object, or from the position of the *"defender"* of the company to be acquired, which resists with all available means and wants to avert this situation;
b) Planning a new market appearance with a new product in a highly competitive market;
c) Solving an organizational problem either as an interface problem regarding the competence or responsibility of two competing areas or in the context of a paradigm shift, e.g., from a line organization to a process-oriented organization.

Admittedly, these examples are very much tied to strategic questions or problems from business practice and are probably not reasonably manageable and "creatively" solvable without business administration knowledge. Therefore, such case studies should always be aligned with the work area of the vacant position so that all interested applicants have a fair chance of success.

For a not entirely serious surprise in the context of an application setting, the implementation of a "projective test" could provide, which is proposed here as the *"Frequency-Color Test"* (see Appendix 2) and is intended for application and supplementation to the applicant interview. Behind this quasi-projective test is the idea that creative or solution-oriented individuals are fundamentally adherents of systems (such as a category system as an order scheme) or of symmetry, which they seek to discover in every task presented to them.

In the construction of a somewhat comparable test, the *"Barron-Welsh Art Scale,"* based on figural drawings with, on the one hand, artists and, on the other hand, non-artists, it turned out that the group of artists preferred drawings that were more complex and asymmetrical, while "the man on the street" preferred more simple-symmetrical drawings. From a stock of approximately 400 figural drawings, 65 drawings could be found that particularly differentiated between the two subgroups (see Barron, 1965, p. 17 ff.). Thus, this finding, confirmed by several studies, would contradict the above assumption unless, for the group of a "normal population," the differences in taste preferences and personality descriptions, as between artists and "ordinary mortals," do not occur or are reversed, which would need to be proven.

An as yet unconfirmed hypothesis would be that such people think about their actions and in this test assign the provided *frequency terms* to the available *colors* with a certain intention or systematics or according to their personal preference. Thus, it would be expected that these individuals would assign the endpoints of the verbal frequency scale, i.e., "never" and "always," with the colors "black" or "white." This choice is intended to express a preference for harmony and balance in the sense of Heider (1958).

Furthermore, another, also not yet confirmed hypothesis would be expected, that rather "emotionally colored people" would warm to a *"cool" color* like "blue" or "green" as a neutral midpoint, and rather rational and analytically thinking individuals would prefer "gray" as a *mixture* of black and white as their center or mix.

Test subjects who cannot engage at all with this task of assigning colors to verbal frequencies, according to this theory, *lack imagination* for a possible system and are also not willing to engage in "mental games." Consequently, they are also less likely to be expected to think and act creatively, as they are reluctant to engage with tasks or requirements that are unfamiliar and not easily understood. Whether the interaction between the left hemisphere for verbal functions (such as frequency indications here) and the right hemisphere for visual representations, depicted and operationalized through color, functions harmoniously or complementarily in these individuals remains an open question.

Admittedly, these conclusions are still very speculative at this stage, but they could contribute to a *negative selection* if empirically confirmed and validated.

4.3 Direct or Indirect Creativity Diagnostics as an Alternative?

A *direct* creativity diagnostics would focus on the operationalization and measurement of creativity as a personality trait or construct. This methodology is mainly supported and implemented through the use of creativity tests or other procedures such as interview questions or case studies (see Sect. 4.2).

One would speak of *indirect* creativity diagnostics if the diagnostics do not rely solely on creative behavior or creative achievements, but also target personality traits that influence creativity, such as curiosity or openness to new experiences, self-confidence, intelligence, risk-taking, etc. In contrast to direct creativity diagnostics, the assessment would not be based solely on the trait facets of creativity but would refer to a "data ring" of various trait scales, which should result in a coherent, i.e., plausible picture according to the chosen and relevant personality theory. In other words, the personality profile of a "creative" (including the trait of creativity) must be plausible and "rounded" and best fulfill the expectation that it is indeed a "creative personality" with adjacent probability.

Methodologically, two approaches are available for this. One is to identify and quantify relationship patterns to other personality attributes through correlation analyses. The other is to calculate the specific influence of these personality factors on creativity as a criterion variable using "Multiple Linear Regression Analyses (MLRA)."

As instruments for the mentioned and potential personality traits (as independent variables), which are likely closely related to creativity, well-known and less-known procedures within the framework of a multiple regression analytical approach would be tentatively offered (see Chap. 7). An MLRA is popular in psychological research, if only to empirically and statistically demonstrate a possible connection, relationship, or effect represented as regression coefficients or weighting factors, between certain indicators, which were determined and selected as trait variables or scales based on a theoretical model, and the independent criterion variable, such as creativity here. Through the regression coefficients of the predictors (such as intelligence), the anticipated influence (or their weight) on creativity as a criterion or outcome variable could later be estimated or approximately predicted. To conclude and illustrate this thought, the trait complexes, such as intelligence, motivation, and personality dispositions, have been listed and presented as influence zones on creativity along with specific personality traits (see Table 4.2).

Alternative or further indicators as possible influencing factors on creativity will be discussed in detail elsewhere, as already indicated (see Chap. 7).

4.4 Creative Diagnostics by "Domains"

Similar to the question of "direct or indirect creativity diagnostics," there is also the problem of the interplay or relationship between different domains within creativity diagnostics. This means that situations in different fields of application can sometimes present themselves very differently and each requires its own investigation concept. Roughly divided, creativity diagnostics can take place in *three* domains (see Fig. 4.1).

Once in *ongoing operations* through observation and assessment of employees and their personnel development from training or induction to their professional deployment. Knowledge acquisition and competence building through learning, practice, and professional experience would be the decisive success parameters in this field of action, which are to be continuously aligned and evaluated for creativity, innovation capacity, or problem-solving skills within the framework of a corporate employee assessment.

A completely different and separate branch would be the *artistic-scientific field*, where it is about elite and sometimes even genius in the sense of extraordinary achievements. In this domain, creativity diagnostics would primarily relate to

Table 4.2 Possible Influence of Selected Personality Traits on Creativity

No.	Trait or Trait Complex	Note or Justification
1	Criterion Variable (DV): *Creativity*	see Sect. 4.1.2
2	Predictors (IV): *2.1 Intelligence* *2.2 Openness to new experiences* *2.3 Curiosity* *2.4 Intrinsic motivation* *2.5 Self-confidence (self-esteem)* *2.6 Risk-taking*	Intelligence is necessary for any problem-solving (including creative achievements) Alternative motivational factors are the drivers for creative behavior and point together in the same direction These two personality dispositions are very strongly related to both personality development and creativity and are understood as "two sides of the same coin"

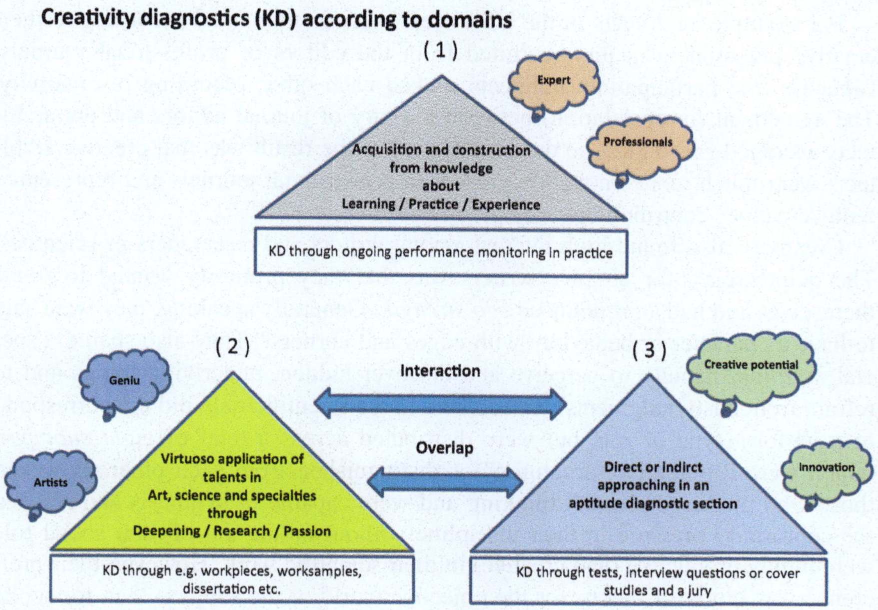

Fig. 4.1 Creativity diagnostics by domains

work evidence, such as pieces of work, scientific contributions, such as a dissertation or the discovery or development of a new active substance.

These procedures have little or nothing to do with the actual *corporate aptitude diagnostics* within personnel selection, depending on the perspective, as creative contributions cannot be easily evoked in aptitude diagnostics. There may be interactions and overlaps both in the objectives and in practice between the mentioned application areas of creativity. Thus, in job-related aptitude diagnostics, one cannot actually speak of creativity diagnostics; at most, vague or approximate statements in the direction of "creativity potential" are possible through methodological measures, such as the application of a creativity test. In this context, it would also be conceivable to ask biographical questions in the interview, such as about the main areas of interest, the number and type of hobbies, and a specific topic that the applicant has intensely dealt with in the past and that still concerns them today. Such questions can at best support and make the assumption of creativity more plausible.

Even in earlier times, there were studies that conducted creativity diagnostics independently of individual persons, but rather preferred aggregated sizes such as domains or other prototypes like professions, etc., and attempted to do so. Barron (1965, p. 58 ff.) referred to a number of studies that attempted, for example, to identify creative individuals in certain *professions* or *disciplines* and to find the most important assessment criteria or personality traits.

For example, architects in the USA were named and ranked according to their creative potential by a jury recruited from the editors of professional journals. Likewise, the participating architects ranked each other according to creativity. The agreement (or correlation) between the jury of journal editors and the architects averaged $r = 0.88$. The decisive factor for the result was that creative architects were much more frequently present in professional journals and represented with "creative" contributions.

Creativity also found high interest among writers and researchers or scientists. The quintessence for creative writers was that they primarily wanted to prove themselves and had a pronounced *ego strength.* Generally speaking, they were said to have a character or behavior "with edges and corners." They also shared a special *intuition,* namely to perceive and discover hidden, underlying things and to refrain from hasty judgments. Researchers in the scientific field did not correspond to a uniform type or role but were distributed across a total of *eight subtypes,* which were differently "structured" or distinguished from each other. However, those who preferred abstract thinking and were capable of synthesis and resisted the conformity pressure in their discipline without falling out of their social role were highly productive (and creative) in their scientific work. However, their preference was more for theory (or the objective world of the subject) than for social life (see Barron, 1965, p. 81 ff.).

4.5 Summary

Creativity diagnostics is, as many probably know, actually "a thing of impossibility." Nevertheless, there have been attempts, particularly in educational diagnostics for schoolchildren and more recently in job-related aptitude diagnostics, to determine and identify creative achievements or creativity potentials, for example, through tests.

For school diagnostics using creativity tests, the results were largely discouraging, as the instruments with their creativity characteristics did not meet psychometric standards, and creativity measurements proved to be method-dependent in the sense of a "material factor." Similar findings were also recorded in a number of validity studies on creativity tests in aptitude diagnostics. Almost without exception, all creativity tests had a "single-factor structure" and lacked differentiated and representative profiles for creativity.

Additionally, almost all operational efforts aimed to diagnose inventiveness or diversity of ideas. Some tests in aptitude diagnostics viewed and subsumed creativity as part of intelligence or another form of conventional thinking, while others closely adhered to a process design.

Particular problems were posed by time constraints, especially in creativity diagnostics using formal procedures such as tests. Such problems, like narrow time windows for task completion, do not afflict, for example, the corporate assessment practice, as supervisors can observe and evaluate creative contributions or performances of their employees over any extended period and must be convinced by them.

Apart from creativity diagnostics in the artistic-scientific field, which in its way offers the possibility to determine "genius" in a specific discipline through work samples or artworks, aptitude diagnostic investigations in applicant selection can at best provide a general ("soft") potential statement or prognosis regarding creativity.

Regardless of the method, whether creativity test, interview questions, or case studies used for aptitude diagnostic purposes, the final assessment of applicants cannot avoid appropriate and prepared evaluation grids or schemes, if only for reasons of necessary "interrater reliability." Preferably, creativity diagnostics should not focus solely on the characteristic of creativity as such but should also rely on other characteristics related to and interacting with creativity, which would benefit the validity assessment. Creativity measurements can thus indirectly, that is, together with other creativity-influencing personality traits, and also differentially diagnostically, approach the construct of creativity. Creativity could then be assessed on the one hand according to various facets and on the other hand according to different task types or challenges. Earlier research activities showed that creativity determination can also be oriented towards overarching or non-individual criteria such as professions or similar.

5 Creativity in Social Interactions and Relationships

After the "creative" handling of factual challenges from the "world of objects" and their open problems, for which creative solutions are sometimes difficult to find, another "playing field" for creative solutions opens up, namely the "social world" with its diverse interpersonal relationships, problems, or conflicts.

Some or even many people may wonder what creativity actually has to do with social behavior, whether in partnerships or relationships or in other interactions on the "social stage." Good ideas or suggestions in social matters or with open problems may help, but "witty ideas" or even inventions, which fundamentally characterize creative achievements, are certainly not to be expected!

With such an attitude, it could easily be forgotten that social situations always occur anew, meaning they do not simply repeat themselves, even if they feel similar, but with their current conditions or imponderables are unique to the people involved. Thus, while disputes between two people may occur frequently, the triggers or causes for them can be completely different each time. Every new situation requires behavior that is appropriate to the situation and original. Such behavior in response to new situational challenges can justifiably bear the designation "creative" in the sense of being novel.

People who always face social challenges in the same way and behave "standardly" and largely consistently usually follow their prejudices, stereotypes, or clichés. They may sometimes or even often be "off track" with their habitual and unreflective reactions and not be successful in resolving social questions or problems. Automatic or stereotypical reactions are anything but creative; rather, they are "dull" and sometimes inappropriate! Not to mention avoiding or evading social encounters due to social anxieties, which are often merely products of imagination or delusions and drive people into social isolation and loneliness.

Those who do not listen to their feelings in the course of their thoughts and actions are also likely to block a significant access to gaining insight. Affective inspirations, also known as intuition, help to become aware of social disturbances, e.g., in communication with a conversation partner, and provide the opportunity

H. Wienkamp, *Creativity Diagnostics*, https://doi.org/10.1007/978-3-662-70432-5_5

to address this and ask for feedback and clarification. Thus, the emotional side also belongs to creativity in social matters, and it gives the cherished thoughts and ideas orientation and "flank protection" due to the accompanying feelings.

To understand the social world, i.e., our fellow human beings and ourselves, each individual forms their own thoughts and dresses them in "social constructions," which consist of their own perceptions, ideas, fantasies, experiences, and sensations and are subjective phenomena. The output of one's own social constructions is not only individually unique but also virtuosic and, if you will, very creative in the sense of being original!

Social constructions are the result of *"social cognitions,"* which arise in the form of mental and emotional processes, such as situational perceptions and interpretations, or personal attitudes like prejudices or stereotypes. Emotional sensations, such as the joy over a sincerely meant compliment, or mental ideas and evaluations also belong to social constructions or cognitions. Not least, the observable intentions and reactions in a person's behavior are also part of social cognitions. Social cognitions further include the self-perception and self-assessment of one's own person in social situations, i.e., "the (own) self."

In order to perceive creatively at all, an individual must first pay sufficient attention to external events. Only perceived external stimuli become "internal representations" according to the "research community." Since apparently most people are optimists, negative or surprising events usually find greater interest, such as a serious accident or a crime (see e.g., Fiske & Taylor, 1991). Unless the events are inherently interesting or appealing, for example, when they "stir up" emotions or create spectacular ideas or images, such as the description of an unusual encounter (e.g., with a public figure like a movie star or top athlete). Different are the "primacy effects" (or in German: pre-induced influences), which pave the way to existing personal evaluation systems and often come into action when certain stimuli are applied with conscious manipulative intent before the actual event. Such perceptions can have both *positive* (e.g., problem sensitization) and *negative* effects (e.g., resistance or reactance) on later problem-solving or creative behavior.

Judgments (conclusions or inferences) are a process that consists of collecting and combining data and information that lead to a judgment or decision. Paying attention to some principles, rules, or insights from cognitive research could help here, although the "artificial world" of experimental laboratories is not necessarily comparable to social reality and usually does not find immediate application there.

In specific situations, normative, scientifically tested rules could be helpful and contribute to avoiding misjudgments, for example, if decision-makers heed that a specific problem situation or event as a single case does not necessarily have to be representative. Under the same conditions, alternative events could also occur, as would be expected with multiple sampling with different results. Analogies also exist to lotteries and games of chance, whose outcomes cannot be determined and can vary greatly, like winning or losing in a lottery or the indeterminate, random change of colors red or black in roulette.

The situation is different when base probabilities exist as frequency indications that allow a certain outcome to be expected with a given probability. Therefore, it is actually incomprehensible that extreme events, which occur very rarely, receive much more attention and are given more credence regarding their possible or repeated occurrence in the future due to their "impact" or strength and their notoriety. This involuntary reaction can be traced back to the *"availability heuristic"* by Kahneman and Tversky (see e.g., Tversky & Kahneman, 1974/2008). According to this heuristic, people spontaneously think of concrete spectacular events when asked about certain occurrences (e.g., they more or less spontaneously recall sensational murder cases or similar when asked about the most common causes of death), which, however, do not occur as frequently as thought.

Creativity in human social behavior can potentially be limitless and continually provide surprises. Creative behavior can particularly occur on the following occasions:

a) Creativity in understanding other people and their social situation
b) Creativity in social manners such as politeness, friendliness, etc.
c) Creativity in maintaining and improving social relationships

Extensive discussions on the models and study results on "social cognitions" are offered, for example, by the textbook by Fiske and Taylor (1991) as well as the textbook of social psychology by Jonas, Stroebe, and Hewstone (Eds., 2014) as a "compendium" of numerous social psychological theories and research findings.

5.1 Creativity in Understanding Other People

To better understand other people, it may require a theory, that is, an idea of intentions and reasons or causes of behavior and their effects on behavior. In this respect, every person relies on inferences, such as "attributions" from the perceived behavior of others. Attributions are nothing more than (speculative) assignments of causes or possible reasons for observed behavior. They may or may not be accurate.

In addition to attributions, evaluation schemas as category systems support people in their attempts to understand social events and draw the right conclusions from them.

5.1.1 Attributions Can Contribute Explanations and Aid Understanding

People tend to attribute either to *internal* reasons inherent in the person, such as character traits, abilities, or even the motivation to do something to behave in a certain way. Or they attribute to external *external* reasons, which are more due to the current situation. This can also be luck or chance. Mental processes can furthermore be oriented either analytically or holistically.—A song, for example, consists of both notes, which are precisely described by musical notation, and a (holistic) melody, as Fiske and Taylor (1991, p. 4) aptly illustrated this "dualism."

Individuals can also be very creative in their explanations or opinions about certain things, events, or developments. However, they often resort to the nearest or a simple explanation, which does not necessarily have to be correct or well thought out and justified. In social psychology, this is referred to as the so-called *"cognitive miser model"* (see e.g., Fiske & Taylor, 1991, p. 13), that is, the *"cognitive miser"* who operates mentally "on a low flame." In principle, this is an avoidance reaction or an escape as protection against mental overload, reminiscent of the research on "hedonistic biases" (Kahneman, 2012), which as "mental quick shots" are the product of "mental laziness" or convenience.

Ultimately, these mechanisms serve to make our social life calculable and predictable, thus manageable, even if occasionally errors or misunderstandings are to be lamented. For this reason, scientific research has made some considerations and developed theories or models to explain these mechanisms. According to Kelley's *"covariation model"* (cited in Fiske & Taylor, 1991, p. 23), social inferences depend on whether

a) a person's observed behavior "X" occurs *exclusively* in a particular situation, for example, if only this person "X" exhibits the behavior;
b) such behavior of the person "X" is *consistent* and always occurs in certain situations (e.g., towards another person "Y");
c) this behavior occurs *independently of the person* and not only towards person "Y" but also towards other people.

Since these *three* conditions can be varied (e.g., according to higher vs. lower expression), at least *eight* "creative" inferences about the observed behavior of the person "X" result.

From research on achievement motivation, the attributions as schemas "internal vs. external causes," "temporally stable vs. unstable," and "controllable vs. uncontrollable" are known and to be added. People use these schemas in the investigation of the causes of success vs. failure in their performances, both in themselves and in others, and use this knowledge for success predictions in the next attempt or endeavor. On the affective level, the *"hope for success"* or the *"fear of failure"* inevitably arises (see Heckhausen, 1963). For the diagnosis of achievement motivation, the *expectation* is, for example, generally a good indicator that can be used for the prognosis of self-assessed performances, especially when the accompanying feelings resonate and are appropriately considered (cf. Fiske & Taylor, 1991, p. 519).

Other research approaches, complementary to or outside of attribution research, therefore focused on the *differences* between the previous expectations about an event and the actual result or current state of this event, and on the (malignant) *deviations from a norm,* which involuntarily initiate or trigger a cause investigation. In the first case, an unexpected defeat in a game causes various speculations about the reasons for the game's outcome when all participants assumed a certain victory. The discovery of a lump in the breast is likely to trigger great fears in a patient that a tumor disease as an abnormality may be present. For clarification and diagnosis, further medical examinations, such as a tissue sample, are promptly necessary, not least at the patient's request.

Apparently, in judgment research experiments, subjects were not able to give sufficient attention and focus to situational circumstances or information when they were either mentally occupied or distracted by "multitasking tasks" or when the events to be judged appeared ambivalent to them. In such situations, the test subjects, as already mentioned, were "cognitive misers" and tended to make rather general or global judgments about the behavioral causes of the target person being evaluated. They would prefer to attribute and reduce the behavior to personality traits, such as the assumption of an aggressive personality or similar, as an explanation. Relaxed subjects incorporated the situationally available information much more into their judgment formation and thus provided an important service and impetus to possible creative ideas or solutions.

People like to assume that their personal opinion or individual behavior in a specific situation is also shared and agreed upon by most other people, which does not necessarily have to be true or accurate. This is referred to as a so-called *false consensus* as a thinking or judgment error, which, as research has shown, is not so rare. This fallacy is particularly prevalent in personal attitudes or opinions that are eminently important to the individual. Or when the situational circumstances are clear, and causation by specific personality factors, for example, embedded in the statement: "He has always been a strange fellow!" is not obvious. For example, fans of a sports club erroneously assume that other people, for instance, in the same place, appreciate their club just as much and show the same enthusiasm as they do. As a result, these individuals lull themselves into a false sense of security that their assessments are universally valid and promote an egocentric perception of social reality (see in detail the explanations, for example, by Fiske & Taylor, 1991)!

A creativity study interested in social events or relationships would play through these various possibilities of causation and try to find both positive approaches to creativity and negative conditions or limitations. Similar to creativity research oriented towards solving factual problems, in social milieus, it is also about the production of good ideas and a "mental agility" or flexibility in thought leadership. While ideas or inspirations usually arise rather spontaneously, flexibility in thinking and acting depends on various personal factors or prerequisites, such as prior knowledge or "emotional memory" (see Sect. 2.2), or on the skillful use of already learned and established evaluation schemas with their respective appropriate categories. Not to be forgotten or ignored are the entrenched and cemented attitude complexes that block or know how to prevent any mobility and willingness to change.

5.1.2 Category Systems Serve Social Orientation and Support Ongoing Assessments

Schemas as self-created classification systems or "implicit personality theories" as assumed and coherent patterns of traits or characteristic profiles additionally complement social cognitions in judgment processes to facilitate social orientation for people. Social schemas are category systems for the classification and evaluation of people or for the interpretation of social situations or observations, comparable to what is generally referred to as *"drawers"* in the sense of categories. *Implicit personality theories* mean the combination of arbitrarily determined personality traits into a coherent pattern, such as: "Who looks good must also be smart!"

Grids or schemas, as they are understood here for social or interpersonal concerns, influence the assessment of other individuals and the *understanding* of social matters, such as problems or conflicts in general, both with their diversity and selection as well as with their firmness or rigidity on the ability to judge. A person with a very limited conception of the "social world," which manifests in the form of rather few schemas as *stereotypes* or *prejudices*, will prefer to perceive and evaluate social situations according to their accustomed grids or stereotypes and with a rather polarizing, thus extreme *"black-or-white thinking"* and will likely lack any creativity. Black-and-white thinking is said to noticeably hinder both human interaction and creativity and flexibility in thinking (see Ullrich & Ullrich, 1982, p. 178). Not to be underestimated is also the massive encrustation or solidification of these schemas, which inevitably conjure up a *rigidity* in attitude and behavior.

Creative would be rather those individuals who possess multiple and more differentiated evaluation schemas, which are also not yet firmly cemented, so that they can view and assess social events from different perspectives with different evaluation systems and are open to new and especially inconsistent information. In short: They master the art of "thinking outside the box" and are not afraid to be infected with new thoughts or perspectives. Thus, they would generally be able to capture their observations once with the help of a suitable category system as a grid and assimilate new suitable observations or experiences, i.e., to incorporate and integrate the new information or insights into their grid. On the other hand, they would be willing to modify their schema through the process of "accommodation" and adapt it to the newly arisen situation if necessary. *Flexibility, learning*, and *willingness to change* would be the attributes that distinguish "creatives" in their social environment and lead them, so to speak, to "new shores." With the help of the psychological mechanisms of *assimilation* and *accommodation*, either the repeated confirmation or necessary adjustment of the self-concept occurs (see e.g., Filipp, 1984).

From social psychological research on "social cognitions," it is also to be contributed here that schemas always depend on the context and therefore must first be developed through everyday life and based on experiences made. People either search for "prototypes" that best or ideally represent the schema to be developed (e.g., a well-known personality from show business as a "role model"), or they orient themselves to a "suitable example" based on previous encounters or experiences and choose a person known to them personally.

Prototypes contain certain more or less accurate characteristics and provide an approximate image or profile of the intended social concept or figure. Feature profiles of prototypes are therefore often blurred and not clearly delineated from one another. Examples from everyday life are usually concrete persons from the past who fill and represent this social category very well, such as "my former class teacher 'X' would be the ideal teacher for me!"

Schemas already contain a category system due to previous experiences and therefore engage more with new information that is supposed to either confirm the system or not! In a schema or category system, the relationships between the features or categories are also already defined and clarified. Social psychology differentiates between various social schemas, such as persons, roles, events, and the self. Category systems emphasize maximum differentiation, i.e., the variability within a class is to be minimized and between the classes or individual categories to be maximized. Fan clubs of a football club will likely see and classify themselves as very similar in their views and beliefs and experience a great agreement among themselves, while they develop an artificially created distance and demarcation to other fan clubs, which they offensively carry outward through their behavior (e.g., when other fan clubs are chosen as the enemy image).

From increasing distance or difference between the categories, stereotypes arise, e.g., as role attributions, which are supposed to facilitate the future recognition process or identification of these typical roles or representatives for the person. Stereotypes or prejudices thus serve and promote self-assurance and contribute to the stability of the schema or evaluation system. Primarily consistent observations are therefore acknowledged, and inconsistent ones are usually or frequently ignored or simply forgotten.

The efforts usually aim to maintain the status quo of a category system, which rather opposes creativity, as new impulses do not penetrate and are not allowed. However, if it is the case that the existing evaluation system can no longer be maintained because it is not practical and carries massive disadvantages or costs, a change or adjustment is likely and no longer excluded. A *"self-fulfilling prophecy,"* which is harmful and counterproductive to the reality of life, would be characterized, for example, by maintaining an unfortunate status quo, whereby the current evaluation schema is artificially, thus unrealistically, confirmed through constant negative experiences. One might think, for example, of the illustrative "scene with the hammer" by Watzlawick (1983/2010), which was based on the erroneous notion of a person that the neighbor would be unwilling to lend the desired hammer and was therefore insulted by the person!—That the reaction of the unjustly accused neighbor exactly corresponded to the "self-fulfilling prophecy" should not remain a secret and not particularly surprise. Without active help from outside with the request and initiation of exactly the opposite experiences, "self-fulfilling prophecies" cannot be eliminated.

Evaluations under time pressure hinder people from seeking and finding evaluation-relevant information, as they use the familiar schema for reasons of efficiency—and possibly prevent creative new solutions. Narrative models as evaluation schemas, which are embedded in a "cover story" that sounds coherent but is not appropriate to the situation, also stand in the way of new insights or experiences, as they have a self-confirming effect. In contrast, scientific models or procedures take new insights or criticism of the status quo seriously for obvious or job-related reasons or out of research interest and are open and ready for creative changes. The search for new insights through the path of falsification, i.e., the search for and exploration or verification of counter-evidence that questions the current state of knowledge or status quo, may already be considered evidence of this. Of course, such self-critical activities are rather uncommon in practice, as they counteract and slow down our cherished and habitual behavioral responses.

Unstable schemas, on the other hand, as already indicated, are not solidified and are receptive to contradictory or inconsistent information. They, so to speak, question themselves as a classification or categorization system, which would be a prerequisite for creative thinking and behavior. Schema changes are, among other things, necessary to overcome "critical life events," such as the death or loss of a spouse or similar, which require a rethinking of the situation for the person concerned and a (successful) "coping" with or in the now impending uncertain future. When pushed to the extreme, or when "push comes to shove," "creatives" are able to completely detach themselves from their acquired evaluation frameworks and focus on the target person as a unique individual in order to perceive and understand them as best as possible. In psychotherapy, this refers to the process of *"focusing"* and *"empathy"* for the client's situation.

Thus, in dependence on their own schemas, creative people differ from non-creative or less creative people in social relationships. It can certainly be assumed that the social understanding of creative people is much more pronounced and accurate.

Before individuals make a personal assessment based on selected personality traits, they have certainly "scanned" the target person according to the roles or stereotypes familiar to them, that is, scrutinized and fixed them. This also includes the assignment to subgroups, which are "creatively" formed if necessary, when, for example, the category "woman" is differentiated and divided into subgroups or subcategories, such as "career woman," because it just fits and imposes itself for this target person to be evaluated.

More ideas could also arise if certain impulses result according to the *"Parallel-Distributed-Processing (PDP) model"* by McClelland et al. (1986; cited in Fiske & Taylor, 1991, pp. 309 ff.). This model assumes scattered items in different schemas instead of sequential process steps, which are activated simultaneously (like "light bulbs" when a light switch is operated), so that new ideas arise due to the possible combinations or constellations.

5.1.3 Creativity in Judgments and Decisions under Uncertainty

Decisions under uncertainty occur especially in social situations, such as the decision to hire a particular applicant or to initially share an apartment and move in together with a life partner. According to research findings on judgments and decisions, people often make misjudgments or wrong decisions when measured against known normative models. Normative models, for example, do not recognize judgment biases due to hedonistic influences, or they ignore other judgment weaknesses, such as the inability to recognize and utilize given relationships as correlations, or, conversely, to assume *"illusory correlations"* that do not exist (see Fiske & Taylor, 1991, pp. 368 ff.).

Now, decision-makers in real situations are exposed to completely different conditions that have relatively little to do with the "ideal-typical" notion of normative models. Normative models, for example, assume constant conditions, i.e., they generally assume the *"ceteris paribus condition"* in all occurring or selected situations, while in the real world "much is in flux" and everything or much is constantly changing. In a dynamic world, decision-makers must be creative and try to act as best as possible and appropriately to the situation according to their ideas. Generally, people only know in hindsight whether their decision or action was right or not, as there were no clues or criteria at the time of the decision that could fulfill and meet an optimality claim in judgment formation. It should also not be forgotten that decisions in reality may also be revisable or correctable if circumstances or the situation demand it, for example, after appropriate feedback from other affected persons.

Such corrective behavior is actually nothing other than "learning from experience"—or, as the saying goes: "Misfortune makes you wise!"

A legitimate question arises in this context: What is creative in understanding other people and their current personal situation, as well as in judgments and decisions in general, and how can this be determined? Whether creativity is the appropriate designation or the "seal of quality" for understanding and shaping a social or interactive process is debatable. Without a doubt, the possibilities of social understanding, judgments, and decisions are very diverse, and they are not always correct and beneficial if false expectations or judgment errors creep in.

Decisions not only relate to the present, the "here and now," but they can also be a conjecture or prediction and gain prognostic significance. "Predictions are difficult, especially when they concern or are supposed to predict the future!" as a frequently used joke expressed and pinpointed this dilemma. For predictions about behavioral reactions, e.g., in social situations, the same problem applies as with the prediction of other, more "tangible" or situational events (e.g., the development of stock prices next year). In all these instances, creativity is especially required in the methodology to arrive at somewhat realistic or very likely accurate predictions.

Cognitive researchers recently revisited the debate by Meehl (1954), which gained fame and attention at the time, between *"clinical judgment"* and *"statistical (or mechanical) judgment"* for diagnosis or predictions in this context (see Kahneman et al., 2023). The *"statistical thinking,"* which compares occurring events with similar processes to identify commonalities or statistical correspondences (such as correlations), is fundamentally different from *"causal thinking,"* which tends to rely on experienced stories or narratives as explanatory patterns (also for future predictions).

Causal thinking, however, is oriented towards the past. It traces the path back from the result to its trigger or cause and attempts to discover an approach or mechanism (e.g., an algorithm) by illuminating the relationships between the process variables. It cannot be denied that causal thinking has a certain similarity with the already known *attributions* (see Sect. 5.1.1) as judgments or causation attributions within the framework of social interactions.

Statistical analyses for judgments and predictions remain true to the mathematical-statistical approach and calculate or quantify existing relationships between the variables under the premise that these relationships are also very likely to persist in the future (which is often correct and occurs). All calculations proceed formalistically and mechanically with the help of mathematics and occur in social situations only for specific purposes and in exceptional situations (e.g., in experiments or surveys). Experts in the field subject their objective or subjective probability expectations (the *a-priori* probabilities) to continuous "updating" using the *"Bayes' theorem"*based on gained experiences, thereby improving their predictions (the *a-posteriori* probabilities).

Probabilistic thinking goes beyond this and integrates *statistical* statements or probability assumptions (such as base probabilities of specific events like diseases or accidents) with *intuitive* assessments based on facts or calculations for (speculative) predictions of any kind. In the simplest case, averaging different observational data would be a likely accurate trend statement about the occurrence of an event or reaction in general, unless other arguments or facts speak against it. For example, it may happen that a supervisor tends to judge *leniently* and gives *good* performance evaluations. The formation of average values is intended to avoid both a one-sided and unintended use of extreme values and to correspond to the "tendency towards the middle" in the repeated occurrence of independent events.

It would be something else to make a *specific prediction* about the suitability or behavior of an individual for a future period, such as a *potential statement* on leadership competence or the recidivism of offenders during their probation. Here, by incorporating base or fundamental probabilities of specific events, such as the recidivism rate of offenders or alcoholics, as well as average considerations based on observed events or samples (e.g., the average success rate in an assessment center for future leaders in the past), a *summary* and a *weighing* against the background of known information would lead to an *intuitive* and hopefully correct prognostic statement, for which there are, however, no guarantees. For such judgment and decision situations, the general behavioral maxim applies: "To the best of one's knowledge and belief!"

In the face of uncertain decisions, creativity, as described, appears in different "guises" and employs a variety of methods for prognostic statements or conjectures about both objective events and the behavior of people in social relationships. Creativity is required as a mental ability, e.g., in the so-called clinical judgment, when the diagnostician "runs out of ideas" and the usual thought directions or concepts no longer help, so new ideas are needed.

5.2 Creativity in Interpersonal Behavior Towards Other People

After understanding social actions or interactions, our fellow human beings expect reactions from us that are appropriate to the situation. Manifest behavior can therefore be correct or also wrong and irritating if it does not meet the expectations of our conversation or interaction partners. It can also reveal itself as simple and straightforward as expected if it does not leave the usual paths and remains calculable or predictable for other people. However, if the reactions cause surprise among our fellow human beings, it can be assumed that creative moments or behavioral traits are at play, which often occur spontaneously and are perceived and experienced as such.

In contrast, *avoidance behavior* would be irritating, especially due to social anxieties. Avoidance behavior could manifest itself as follows:

a) Pretending not to be there, i.e., deliberately "making oneself small" through "absence displays" (Ullrich & Ullrich, 1978, p. 47).
b) When someone "holds back" their opinion and says nothing about it.
c) If one always assumes the worst to avoid unpleasant surprises, aligns one's behavior a priori to it, and gives in to fatalism, so that, for example, one does not have to exert oneself excessively to achieve the goal.

The cause of avoidance behavior is usually *"the fear of fear,"* which not only leads to social isolation but is essentially also self-deception because the resulting behavior is not desired and will certainly be regretted later.

Besides the special "special cases," namely on the one hand offering and providing help, on the other hand attempts at manipulation to pursue and realize self-serving goals (see Sects. 6.2 and 6.3), there are many other behaviors in dealing and communicating with other people. Which "social worlds" are to be considered here, and where creative behavior tendencies might be expected, can be seen in Fig. 5.1.

According to this scheme, interpersonal interactions can initially be differentiated as a social milieu into a *private* and a *public* sector. Certainly, it makes a difference in communication whether a problem is resolved within the family or whether one is discussing, for example, a contentious parking violation with a municipal official at the regulatory office, which would also be its own, so-called domain. Depending on the quality of the arguments, behavior can be judged as

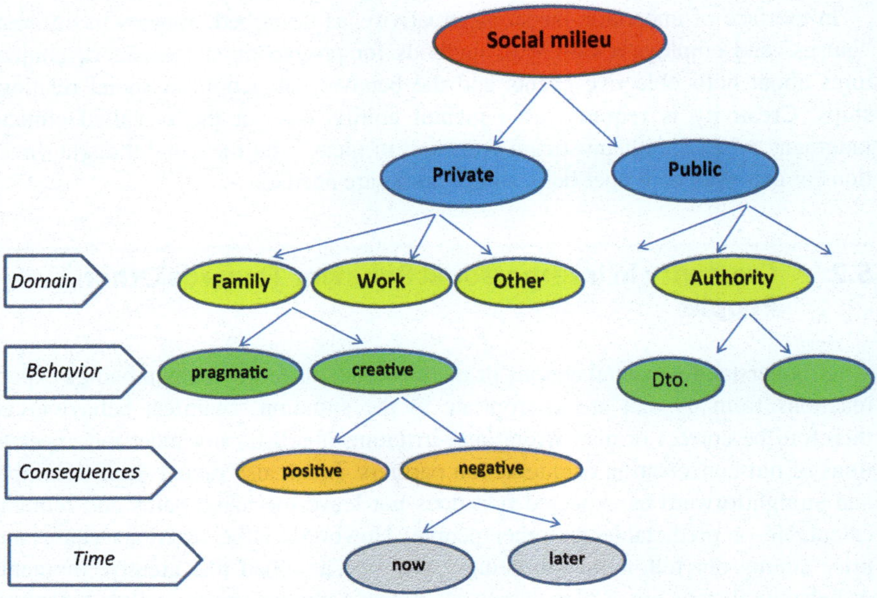

Fig. 5.1 Framework for the study of creativity in social milieus

either *pragmatic* or *creative* (in the case of extraordinary or surprising arguments). Sometimes verbal expressions also depend on the expected *positive* or *negative* consequences and the planned *timing* of the reaction, as suggested and depicted in this scheme. All in all, this scheme serves as a plan or action strategy and can accordingly also be used for diagnostic purposes.

With the areas "private" vs. "public" included in Fig. 5.1 and the domains functioning as subgroups that represent the social context for individual behavior, the *roles* or *functions* addressed in the social schemata have also been considered.

According to the situational understanding concerning the perceived behavior of a target person (see Sect. 5.1), a personal reaction or a behavior intention tied to one's own needs follows more or less arbitrarily and automatically, which leads to an action strategy and corresponds to or considers the criteria or conditions listed in Fig. 5.1. Of course, the already mentioned attributions as presumed causes of the perceived behavior as well as one's own category or evaluation systems are guiding.

From an entirely objective perspective, behaviors are initially situation-dependent, which, by the way, is neither a new nor a surprising insight. Thus, people are friendly to others, for example, not only because they are inclined towards another person and show them sympathies and therefore are always or predominantly friendly to him (or her), but also when the situation calls for friendly behavior and is predestined for it. For example, if I ask another person for a favor, friendliness would certainly be appropriate and beneficial in my own interest.

According to the findings of social psychological research, the behavior currently exhibited does not necessarily have to correspond with internal attitudes or personality development. It is even assumed to be completely independent (a "zero correlation") if the two psychological areas operate on different levels. On the one hand, it is true that attitude complexes or personality traits are generally more broadly defined, while behavior tends to adapt to and react to the current situation. On the other hand, psychological influencing factors such as attitudes, etc., operate on the cognitive level, while in concrete behavior, current feelings also resonate and give the behavior an "affective flavor." This dualism is comparable to the goal projections arising from cognitions, while needs usually express an affective component (see also Fiske & Taylor, 1991, pp. 517 and 522).

Finally, the observable behavior also depends on a person's behavior control, that is, on the so-called *monitoring* and the chosen preferences or control principles. Some people ask themselves in every social encounter how they should ideally behave and thus align themselves very strongly with adopted social norms, such as the expectations or needs of their conversation or interaction partners. Since their conversation partners logically change from situation to situation, these individuals must be erratic and inconsistent in their behavior patterns. Behavioral flexibility, to put it positively, is a sign of high and pronounced "self-monitoring" in such people. Other people remain more true to themselves and align their behavior with their self-concept without regard to the current situation and their fellow human beings, for which low self-monitoring is more likely to be the cause (see Fiske & Taylor, 1991, p. 534).

To be added are misalignments such as the assumption that other people operate from different norms and that deviations inevitably lead to conflicts or irritations, and therefore automatically devalue or reject the interaction partner, which generates *fear of rejection* in him (or her). Or the assumption of *irrational expectations* of other people towards oneself is extremely critical, as they provoke misconduct with very negative consequences for oneself, such as disappointment, alienation, or overstrain (see Ullrich & Ullrich, 1982, p. 27).

Human creative behavior is thus dependent on many social influencing factors, with understanding (see Sect. 5.1) providing the fundamental "setting of the course."

5.3 Creativity in Social Relationships

Creativity in social relationships is far from just a joint (creative) leisure activity. Social relationships, such as a marriage or partnership, remain intact even if the paths sometimes necessarily diverge, as each partner, for example, pursues their own profession, possibly at a different workplace, or if the partners enjoy different hobbies, so they are not constantly together even in their leisure time. In other social relationships, such as friendships or acquaintanceships, the "separation" may be even more extensive, as people, especially outside of good acquaintanceships, still want to have their own private life and place great value on it.

Whether marriage, partnership, friendship, or just acquaintance, in any case, two important, if not "strategic," decisions are at hand: Namely, on the one hand, a selection of partners must be made, and on the other hand, within an existing relationship, one must "invest" in the relationship if it is to continue to exist!

Partners may more or less randomly "cross paths," for example, due to a formal introduction by other people or due to a spontaneously arising conversation (e.g., as small talk). From such encounters, an acquaintance and then a relationship can develop quite casually. Some people, on the other hand, have recently been using so-called dating portals and are specifically looking for possible partnerships—probably with varying success both in the initial contact and in relationship maintenance!

Within existing relationships, creativity is certainly required if, to put it colloquially, the partner is to be "kept in a good mood." This not only concerns joint leisure activities or other joint ventures, such as planning and realizing an elaborate larger vacation or adventure trip to exotic countries, but also extends to "deeper layers" up to existential questions, such as entering into a marriage or life partnership.

To paraphrase the already cited model (see Fig. 5.2) by Heider (1958), every social relationship requires both stability and balance if it is to be harmonious and satisfactory.

According to this model of a *"triangular relationship"* (Wienkamp, 2022b, p. 94), it is clearly evident that both partners must like each other and have a positive attitude towards the shared relationship, which promises harmony and relaxation. However, the prerequisite for this well-being is that the many interpersonal problems and conflicts, especially in committed relationships, are resolved in a manner satisfying to both parties, both in ordinary everyday situations and due to particular relationship-damaging character traits or behaviors. At the very least, it

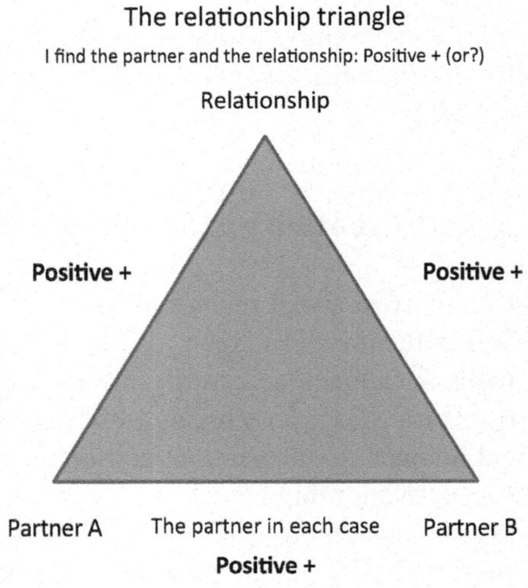

Fig. 5.2 The relationship triangle. (According to Heider's balance theory, 1958)

is expected that a process of improvement has been initiated. Not only does the quality of the relationship benefit from an intact social relationship, but both partners would also be able to draw additional strength and power from this relationship and effectively use their personal resources with the help of their resilience, or resistance, in coping with normal everyday life or overcoming so-called critical life events.

An insight into the therapy forms developed for this purpose may provide an understanding of which communication and behavioral problems are to be expected in a partnership and how to address them ("creatively") (see e.g., Mandel et al., 1979). Problems as well as the content of such communication or couple therapies are primarily social anxieties, aggressions, dominance or power posturing, excessive control behavior, communication deficits, lack of affirmation, or lack of positive reinforcement of mutual behavior. Not least, self-esteem issues also play into the relationship, which may have occurred as experienced traumatic events even before the relationship, or a degrading or otherwise inappropriate parenting style in the parental home could be responsible for acquired inferiority complexes or similar issues.

Inferiority problems as well as social anxieties are a burden for a relationship and are difficult to endure in the long run. For example, dealing with fears, as is expressed daily in a committed relationship or in communication or couple therapy, also fuels "creative endeavors," albeit in a negative or destructive sense, to bypass or avoid an open approach to the underlying problems or "primal conflicts." Unresolved conflicts from the past (such as early childhood) lead, according to psychoanalytic theory, through the psychological mechanism of *transference* to *"reaction formations,"* as the repressed emotional problems seek a channel or outlet and, for example, are "projected" onto another person (e.g., the partner), making this person inexplicably become the "scapegoat."

Social relationships, whether in everyday normal life, such as in the domestic sphere, or in couple therapy (see e.g., Mandel & Mandel, 1979, p. 13 ff.) as a "last resort" out of the crisis, are subject to the requirement of continually seeking and finding new ways to address and resolve existing relationship problems or conflicts. However, it is better for both partners to prevent them and thus achieve a relaxed and harmonious relationship.

The counter-model to this would be a latent or openly expressed dissatisfaction, either interspersed with arguments and unproductive discussions or with constant brooding over why the relationship with the partner is so unsatisfactory.—Obviously, in such a situation, "some switches have been set incorrectly," and fundamental conditions of harmonious coexistence have not been sufficiently considered. A communication or couple therapy is then a way out or a recipe when things are not going well in a relationship and would serve as a catalyst for improvement. It is something like a tutoring session through the use of a learning program tailored to the relationship problem, with the goal of practicing *metacommunication* in particular. With the gradual success of metacommunication, the couple achieves the therapy goal and goes well-prepared and ready "into freedom" or independence.

According to most psychotherapists, the key to a better shared life in a relationship is *"discrimination learning"* (see e.g., Mandel & Mandel, 1979, p. 31). Adequate differentiation helps a partner in their spontaneous reactions in specific critical situations as well as in behavior control, for example, to address unpleasant feelings or experiences with the use of important positive or negative reinforcers. Primarily, behavior therapy has dealt with the mechanisms of conditioning, i.e., the practice or habituation of behaviors or behavior modification, and has provided therapists with an extensive "toolkit." Its arsenal includes "tools" such as response hierarchies, primary and secondary reinforcers, reinforcement schedules, and conditions of generalization, which they can and should use "creatively."

From the therapy school of the *"Assertiveness Training Program (ATP)"* (according to, for example, Ullrich & Ullrich, 1980, 1982), it should be added that in "discrimination learning," it is about learning new behaviors on the one hand, and unlearning unwanted harmful reactions on the other. Interventions such as a "thought stop" provide assistance, for example, to interrupt an existing connection between a thought or a negative expectation and the subsequent sensation as an anxiety reaction. It would also be helpful to recognize when a collective solution is indicated because one's own power is insufficient and limited, and when a partnership solution as a balance of interests between two equal parties is appropriate. The concrete behavior on the "emotional track" should be accompanied by a decisive "assertiveness" with, for example, the statement: "I insist that…" and not by aggressions such as tirades, which only mark the current helplessness and self-insecurity. The person should also not be irritated or distracted by other present individuals who experience disadvantages due to the shown behavior in connection with the justified concern, such as having to wait and reacting irritably and possibly with indignation (see Ullrich & Ullrich, 1980, p. 174 f.).

In view of the fact that human learning predominantly takes place in social situations or life circumstances, it is impossible for individuals to communicatively *"not"* react to social events or verbal expressions, as psychological science propagated a long time ago (see Watzlawick et al., 1982). Likewise, it is not possible to *"not"* react or *"not"* manipulate (see Wienkamp, 2023b) when specific behavioral maneuvers with, for example, reinforcement intentions are indicated. Incidentally: Even silence is a reaction!

Learning is then demonstrated in the discrimination of showing behavior appropriate to the situation and, for example, positively reinforcing or rewarding the partner's behavior at the right moment or, conversely, ignoring and negatively reinforcing it to extinguish it. Thus, not only must giving praise be learned, but the target person must also recognize and appreciate it as praise. For praise to stabilize as recognition within a social relationship as a positive reinforcer and occur more frequently in the future, a positive feedback to the praiser must necessarily come from the target person. Under no circumstances should the praised person relativize or even devalue praise with a remark like *"That was not worth mentioning or a matter of course for me,"* thereby expressing: *"I did not deserve the praise at all"* (cf. Ullrich & Ullrich, 1980, p. 37).

Success learning at the end of the chain means nothing other than that these behavioral reactions are more or less involuntarily used later due to positive feedback and lead to "self-reinforcement" and generalization.

Sometimes therapy also requires the (creative) intervention of the therapist when he (or she) deliberately points out *"double binds"* and then provokes according to all the rules of the "therapeutic art," such as with the remark: *"You argue so much because you love each other"* (Watzlawick et al., 1982, p. 236), thereby deliberately evoking reactance from the couple, for example, as resistance in the form of stopping arguing out of protest. Alternatively, a creative intervention can also consist of consciously and deliberately practicing arguing on therapeutic order—as a so-called "paradoxical intervention"!

Incidentally, conflict is often the result of "defective" character traits that are fully expressed or revitalized within the relationship. The striving for dominance due to power desires is, for example, a form that oppresses the partner and makes life together difficult if he (or she) does not want to be the oppressed or loser in this imposed game from the outset. An aberration of power abuse is also an excessive control behavior that the "control freak" likes to use to demonstrate to his or her partner that he (or she) is not competent and complete, but dependent on others. Sometimes power or control people use the mechanism of the *"self-fulfilling prophecy,"* by reluctantly granting their partner a certain (pseudo-) independence on a suitable occasion, but then unsettling him or her so much that his or her initial attempts fail, and they feel confirmed and boast with their already formed prejudice of having been right.

Harmful and perverse for a relationship is also the use of "trigger or signal words" such as the word "actually" or similar, which not only create a negative undertone but also indicate a problematic, little-trusted relationship that "drives the recipient up the wall," i.e., negatively emotionalized by anger. Creative remedy is not only the conscious omission of such trigger words but also an awareness of the form of expression, i.e., the nonverbal communication through facial expression or body language, true to the motto: *"A picture is worth a thousand words."* Should misunderstandings arise in this context, it remains for the communication partners, preferably in therapy, to explain their adopted nonverbal expression with words.

5.4 Possibility of Creativity Assessment in Social Relationsships and Situations

For creativity diagnostics in social relationships, this generally has the consequence that attention must be directed towards the obstacles and destructive behavior patterns that oppose creativity, in order to then see which creativity potentials could arise from overcoming them. Methodologically, this is done through a *behavior* or *problem analysis* created within the framework of psychodiagnostics (see Bartling et al., 1980, 2016).

From the design principles to skillful implementation, it is sometimes a tedious and longer path, especially when previous habits are not abandoned and no new creative attempts to alleviate or solve the problem have been tried. In many cases, social problems have already been established in childhood, for example, through an inappropriate or insensitive parenting style.

Even children were exposed to incorrect parenting methods in their parental home and were indoctrinated with unfortunate attitudes as behavioral principles, which they have to "crack," i.e., suffer from, their entire lives. An example is an *ambivalent* communication style, which served to disguise and conceal one's own interests and always keep open the possibility of denial or evasion. Later partners then do not know what the other wants and intends, and despair over it or resort to rebellion or open resistance, causing the relationship crisis to escalate (see Mandel & Mandel, 1979, p. 53 ff.).

Thus, as a result of a diagnostic investigation, it should become clear that a "turn for the better," whether outside or during couple therapy, must start with communication behavior. Numerous examples from practice serve on the one hand as negative examples of how communication should not be, such as creating so-called *double binds*, where the other partner can only react incorrectly and despair, as he or she always loses, no matter which behavior he or she alternatively chooses and shows (see Mandel & Mandel, 1979, p. 274). On the other hand, it is important to mobilize creative resources to find a way out of the crisis. Much depends on the following virtues: *mutual positive appreciation* (including self-esteem), *being genuine* or *self-congruence*, i.e., being authentic and ensuring a match between inner attitude and external behavior, and the *verbalization of emotional experiences* to exclude ambivalences or misunderstandings.

Being authentic or natural in communication also means being courageous and not deliberately omitting taboo topics, even if it is difficult and potentially unpleasant surprises threaten. There is likely a creative learning need to recognize that in certain situations a conversation about the relationship itself needs to be conducted, and to demonstrate what is known and functions as "metacommunication." To put it in the words of Mandel and Mandel (1979, p. 127): "Two things must be learned: First, to request *feedback* from the other to clarify how an ambiguous message should be understood; second, to provide *paraphrases* of social perceptions ('I have the feeling you might want to tell me…' or 'I might have wanted to express…')."

However, feedback must also be learned by the partners to avoid being misunderstood through veiled or ambivalent responses. The more effort is invested in this, the more the creativity of social communication is stimulated and promoted (see Mandel & Mandel, 1979, p. 134).

The goal and purpose of psychological diagnostics is therefore to determine the exact status quo or current state of creative resources or, conversely, behavioral deficits, in order to derive the necessary measures from the comparison with a target or ideal state. With a professional behavior analysis by a licensed and experienced psychotherapist, all necessary diagnostic information should be obtained or deduced.

Problem or behavior analyses identify the negative triggers for maladaptive behavior with either suffered or expected negative consequences by collecting and establishing a "behavior chain"—also known and represented as a "behavior equation." *Condition analyses*, on the other hand, are dedicated to the exploration and analysis of social structures in interpersonal relationships and their interactions. Often, the hierarchical structure of an organization (e.g., an authority) and the entrenched habits and customs shape the communicative and interactive behavior of employees (e.g., officials in an office or administration) towards their clients or customers in "face-to-face situations," as they are both committed to their role or function and responsible to their superiors for their actions and their consequences. Thus, the responsibility or cause of specific behavior would shift away from personality dispositions and intentions to the situational or organizational conditions owed to the prevailing environment.

With a condition analysis, it would also be clarified which feelings (e.g., fear of disappointment) preceded a specific event or behavior, in order to understand the subsequent, resulting feeling (e.g., anger or annoyance) in oneself (see Ullrich & Ullrich, 1982, p. 69).

In addition to direct social contacts in relationships or similar, there is also creative acting or behavior towards an anonymous audience or the public, for example, when an artist, while creating their artwork, already thinks about the critics in the relevant gazettes or in the feuilleton section of a daily newspaper and plans their possible reactions. For some social science researchers (such as Glaveanu, 2022, p. 37 ff.), it is beyond doubt that the addressed "public opinion" contributes to the emergence of creativity in our culture. In principle, what takes place is what can be described as an exchange of ideas or thoughts for mutual learning, which repeatedly provides new creative stimuli in social dialogue. In this context, the new social media should not be forgotten, which, with the help of the internet, enable entirely different forms of mutual exchange of thoughts or ideas and joint learning (see, for example, Henriksen et al., 2022, p. 327 ff.).

The exchange of opinions propagated here between, for example, an artist and their audience via social media is very reminiscent of a variant of creativity training, namely *brainstorming,* where it is also about improving the status quo of an idea or a present proposal through other participants.

Statistical information, to name just a few indicators exemplarily, which also have diagnostic value, would be, for example, a frequency evaluation of the *"clicks"* like *"like or dislike,"* which at least provide an idea of the feedback on the presented contributions or new creative ideas. With the time measurement of staying on a website, the interest in this contribution can also be read and quantified.

5.5 Summary

Wanting to determine creativity in social relationships or in a social context is likely to meet with a divided, if not even astonished, response. This is quite understandable and comprehensible in principle, because, to my knowledge, no procedures or studies have been developed or created under the designation "*creativity assessment for social relationships*" or similar. Naturally and understandably, the individual competence to solve relationship disturbances and social conflicts found sufficient interest.

Nevertheless, it is not wrong to search for creative or virtuosic approaches in the social or interpersonal interactions and events listed here and to allow oneself an insight as well as an outlook. Both the understanding of our fellow human beings and the subsequent reactions towards them can, on the one hand, be stereotypical, but they can also be very varied and adapted to the situation, which certainly benefits the quality of the relationship.

Through a professionally conducted behavior or problem analysis, the relationship problems should have been clearly identified and "on the table," so that both the relationship disturbances and existing communication deficits, which have so far prevented a harmonious relationship, can be addressed and resolved in a "creative" way. Sometimes this requires the help or support of communication or couple therapy or an ATP aimed at building and practicing self-assured behavior.

In principle, creativity diagnostics consist both in a "negative diagnostics," when there is a lack of effective actions within a relationship, and in a positive approach to discover, for example, previously unused, buried creativity potentials and to use them successfully, for example, in the context of therapy or a self-help group.

Positive creative impulses can arise when, within the framework of a social dialogue, the public or an interested audience is also taken into account and asked for their opinion by the actors such as artists, scientists, etc. Due to the existence of social media used by everyone, such as the internet, it has become easy to engage in creative exchange of ideas with offers of ideas and feedback from either a known or anonymous audience and to benefit from the contributions and resonance of others, as in brainstorming. Additionally, some relevant information about the interest shown and social resonance can be gained through statistical parameters.

6 Motivational Factors in Social Relationships and Interactions

Research activities in social psychology contributed insights and findings alongside scientific investigations into "social cognitions," which, although not directly related to creativity, come into contact with creative behavior *indirectly* through selected personality-specific influencing factors. One might consider the motivation for attachment, which can more or less also be a prerequisite for helpfulness. In attachment or affiliation motivation, as with other psychological constructs, it is important to explore the psychosocial causes operating in the background. On the other hand, social relationships are heavily dependent on, or are significantly shaped by, rather opposite behavioral tendencies to attachment motivation, namely self-interest, which manifests in selfish behavioral traits. Small group research (or group dynamics), which touches on team building, has become known and popular, among other things, through various creativity techniques such as brainstorming.

In contrast to social cognitions, which trigger and force a rather mental process, these research contributions have a much stronger behavioral reference, both mentally (or cognitively) and emotionally, as they specifically address the communication or interaction behavior of individuals.

6.1 Attachment Motivation

Attachment motivation (or: affiliation) is one of the three motivational factors in McClelland's model (e.g., 1987), alongside achievement motivation and the pursuit of power. Similar to McClelland, various researchers took up this construct and attempted to link it with other psychological characteristics related to the natural human tendency to form close relationships or at least make contact with other people, and to investigate connections. Whether attachment motivation is related to creativity in any way is not immediately apparent.

H. Wienkamp, *Creativity Diagnostics*, https://doi.org/10.1007/978-3-662-70432-5_6

Mehrabian and Ksionsky (1974) conducted several experimental studies based on a behaviorist approach to primarily investigate the influence of

a) a dependency on other people,
b) fear of rejection by others ("sensitivity of rejection")
   as well as
c) conformity pressure ("conformity") and
d) ingratiation through overly attentive behavior ("ingratiation")

on attachment motivation through questionnaire surveys and role-playing, with the distinction of whether the social encounters involved a good and familiar acquaintance or a previously unknown stranger.

As a result, it can be noted that attachment motivation positively influences contact behavior in social situations, as the participants in the experiment had a positive attitude towards their interaction partner or developed one during an encounter in a waiting position, which positively affected their communication and also their final evaluation of the social situation they had just experienced with their communication partner. According to *"social reciprocity"*, their conversation partner reciprocated their positive and courteous behavior in the same way, according to their assessment.

Socially anxious individuals with extreme sensitivity to social rejection by their contact partners behaved quite insecurely in their social behavior and felt overall uncomfortable and stressed in this situation, which made them dissatisfied on the one hand, and on the other hand, this negative aura affected and transferred to the reactions of their social partner.

In a *social dependency*, the motive "forming social contacts or relationships" fulfilled a help or protection function, as the affected individuals hoped to compensate for their own insecurity or fear through social relationships and to improve their social situation.

Social dependency and conformity in behavior are revealed when someone says "yes" to everything and is willing to unconditionally adapt to and submit to other people. Such individuals generate *approach behavior* due to attachment or affiliation efforts to supposedly improve their own well-being and to compensate for personal deficits. Social fears, due to feared rejection or dismissal, are negative reinforcers that contribute to *avoidance behavior* and thus to the prevention of social bonds or relationships. In these opposing behavioral tendencies, these emotional forces act independently of each other, as confirmed by correlation calculations with a tendency towards zero correlation.

Ingratiation with other individuals, like attachment motivation, also initially has a positive effect on the emotional world of those involved in social relationships. Unfortunately, it is a sign of a one-sided dependency of a person on another person, while attachment motivation is supported by a certain self-confidence.

A diagnosis of attachment motivation helps to identify those individuals who are particularly skilled (or even creative) in social behavior, easily find access to other people, and engage in pleasant conversations with them. Attachment motivation and, consequently, empathy can therefore be considered so-called *therapist variables*, as they embody exactly what counseling or therapy requires (cf. Mehrabian & Ksionsky, 1974, p. 155 ff.).

For an (unpublished) project work in 2015 with 60 participants as part of a doctoral study in psychology, in which the author of this publication was personally involved, the influence of reward and punishment sensitivity and *"attachment style"* on social behavior was to be investigated. Social behavior was defined as *"agreeableness"* according to the Big Five personality trait (see Sect. 7.1.2), and the reward and punishment sensitivity was operationalized using the *BIS and BAS scales* by Carver and White (1994; for further explanation see Sect. 7.2.3).

In this project work, attachment style corresponded to certain variants of attachment motivation according to the characteristics of the German-language *"Attachment Style Questionnaire (ASQ)"* by Hexel (2004) and their operationalization as trait scales:

(1) Trust ("secure") as a sign of security
(2) Discomfort with closeness ("insecure or fearful") as a sign of social anxiety
(3) Need for approval ("preoccupied A") as a sign of dependency
(4) Preoccupation with relationships ("preoccupied B") as a sign of general concern
(5) Neglect of relationships ("dismissing") as a sign of indifference or disinterest

In the original English version, there were *four* attachment styles, which, for example, Nikitin and Freund (2010) referred to in a similarly designed study with the influence of these attachment styles as IV and three different forms of *social approach and avoidance motivation* as a mediator on *"interaction anxiety"* and attempted to analyze and clarify the existing relationships using a "structural equation model (SEM)".

According to current research, the attachment styles follow the following dimensions: (1) *anxiety* and (2) *avoidance,* which in combination (and with bipolar polarity) lead to the also four attachment styles (a) *secure,* (b) *preoccupied,* (c) *fearful* and (d) *dismissing* (see e.g., Karremans & Finkenauer, 2014, p. 408).

In this project work, only the designated signal items or marker variables from the *ASQ* by Hexel (2004) were extracted and used as attachment styles and—due to the relatively small number of items (18 items)—summarized and reinterpreted into an *"ambivalent attachment style"* that now contained both items with *positive* and *negative* statements as behavioral tendencies.

As expected, the trait "Behavioral Inhibition System (BIS)" as a symptom of anxiety and conflict avoidance correlated highly significantly positively with the (self-assessed) "agreeableness," which expressed a certain restraint in behavior and in engaging in conflicts. The "Behavioral Approach System (BAS)" as a symptom of reward sensitivity, on the other hand, correlated negatively, but (still) not statistically significantly with "agreeableness," which seemed plausible, as the trait BAS involves demands or desires towards others in social situations, thus a rather "offensive social behavior." The "ambivalent attachment style" constructed here also correlated positively with "agreeableness," although not yet significantly, but highly significantly with the BIS, which suggests an *inhibition* in social situations towards other people with an ambivalent attachment style. In the multiple linear regression analysis (MLRA), the *BIS* achieved a standardized regression coefficient (Beta) of 0.499 ($p < 0.001$) and thus had a strong influence on "agreeableness," while the trait scales *BAS* and "*ambivalent attachment style*" showed a non-significant negative effect, which was plausible due to the indicated direction (because of the negative sign). The MLRA model was highly significant ($p < 0.002$) and explained 19% of the variance or variability of the results. With only 60 participants in this study, who used the waiting time in a psychotherapeutic practice to fill out the questionnaire, this result was appropriate and quite promising.

In view of the existing studies on attachment motivation, due to the positive or negative reinforcements in making contact or communicating with other people, attachment motivation would be a good prerequisite for the development of creativity, especially when social situations (e.g., in a workgroup or team) are experienced as relaxed and satisfactory.

6.2 Conditions and Possibilities of (Creative) Willingness to Help

Showing willingness to help is, as psychological research has found, probably not a matter of course. It is not immediately apparent how this behavioral disposition connects with creativity and manifests itself in altruistic behavior. It should be self-evident that if creativity influences the willingness to help, at least a natural inclination towards creativity is assumed, and creativity ensures imaginative virtuosity and a positive basic attitude that supports a general motivation to help.

The willingness to provide help is counteracted by "*diffusion of responsibility,*" also called "*collective non-responsibility,*" as studies in social psychology have empirically confirmed, for example, in accidents or disasters. The more bystanders were present at the accident as spectators, the *less* willing they were to make an emergency call or provide "first aid," as everyone tends to rely on others according to the findings (see, for example, the studies by Latane & Darley, 1968; cited in Levine & Manning, 2014, p. 369 f.).

In the experimental studies conducted on this topic, the willingness to make an emergency call and actively intervene in the event of a (supposed) epileptic seizure of a test participant (as a confederate of the experimenter) was simulated depending on the number of test subjects. The more bystanders were present at the event, the *more passive* the reaction to the incident became, or the *smaller* the proportion of emergency signals.

In contrast, it is considered positive that a good mood is supposed to promote willingness to help. When expecting emotional recognition or reward as "positive reinforcement," help is more likely to be given than in the presence of guilt feelings, which are known to prevent or hinder the emergence of a good or cheerful mood (cf. Fiske & Taylor, 1991, p. 440). With their help, helpers apparently want to do something good for themselves and earn positive feedback or gratitude.

Ultimately, showing willingness to help is a question of motivation, which, however, according to the findings of social psychological research, is overshadowed by some essential conditions. Thus, motivation or will alone is not enough if the means or competence to help, i.e., *the ability*, is not present and simply lacking. It is not always about helping an elderly frail person cross a busy street, which any individual can undoubtedly do, but often effective help also requires a certain professionalism, for example, in the application of a technique or craft that not everyone naturally masters. Such a shortcoming or deficit cannot be "made up for" or compensated for, even with a great deal of creative talent. It is also generally said: *"Well-intentioned is not the same as well-executed!"*

Another barrier to not being able to help would be the *not being allowed,* i.e., a prohibition or a ban on showing willingness to help. Ignoring such prohibitions is likely to be associated with expected negative personal consequences. For example, in wartime, it is strictly forbidden and punishable for the local population to help prisoners of war or other needy "enemies" and to provide them with food or the like.

Human willingness to help is not only a question of ability, but the willingness and action also depend on *sympathy* or *antipathy* towards the target person, as analyzed by Heider (1958, p. 122) at the time, and the affective and personal consequences for the prevailing relationship quality were elaborated:

a) An investment in the relationship is thus any help provided if the two people like or find each other sympathetic.
b) A lack of help due to the helper's inability is generously forgiven among mutually appreciative (sympathetic) people and does not harm the relationship.
c) In a relationship based on antipathy, help that is not possible due to a lack of competence (or know-how) meets with indifference.
d) Refused assistance that would have been quite possible and feasible is damaging to the relationship in all cases, as this omission of help is perceived by the person in need as intentional and deliberate punishment or disregard. If, in addition, the two people "do not get along," i.e., do not like each other, the refused help would further promote the prevailing antipathy and existing animosities, and the poor relationship quality would escalate even further. In contrast, among previously sympathetic people, a massive conflict arises that still needs further clarification!

Willingness to help generally knows no boundaries or restrictions and can occur in very different ways, such as direct help with a problem, through donations, or through voluntary, charitable activities. Whether one can speak of a creativity diagnosis in the true sense in this context remains an open question. Nevertheless, it must be considered that the various forms of willingness to help are subject to certain limitations and restrictions that can set boundaries to diversity and virtuosity and also to potential creativity.

6.3 Selfish Tendencies in the Exercise of Creativity

In addition to the helpfulness already discussed, selfishness, also known and familiar under the more euphonious term *"self-interest"*, is considered the essential motivational force for creative achievements and behavior. Selfishness is a natural disposition that serves the purpose of securing existence and survival in the wild. Offensive and worthy of criticism are selfish excesses, which manifest both in displayed behavior and in an unrestrained and unchecked *greed* (e.g., for money and possessions).

According to Lersch (1938), selfishness can be depicted and defined as a personality factor on a *bipolar* dimension with the endpoints *"selflessness (altruism)"* and *"selfishness"*. In the middle of this personality dimension, there would be a state of equilibrium as a *natural* or *"healthy" selfishness*. The existence of a "natural selfishness" is supported by social researchers such as Miller (1999). For them, selfishness is, on the one hand, a psychological mechanism that functions as protection and responsiveness in the face of impending personal *disadvantages,* such as through deception or fraud, and is necessary. On the other hand, it is entirely legitimate from a scientific and social perspective to act in one's own interests and to arrive at a *beneficial* decision for oneself through calculation and weighing of pros and cons (e.g., costs versus gains).

Incentives and risks also affect self-interests when obstacles or barriers stand in the way of achieving certain personal goals and may prevent goal attainment. According to the studies by Wienkamp (2017, 2020a), there can be both *positive* escalation effects between the personality traits of *incentive motivation* and *risk propensity* when a higher incentive leads to more risk-taking, as well as *negative* interaction effects or interplays regarding risky decisions or behavior when a desired object functions as an incentive, but the circumstances rather signal and suggest caution or risk aversion in concrete behavior due to unknown or possible dangers or undesirable side effects.

To address and master these dilemmas in decisions and behavior, creativity can sometimes help or is even required. Many (creative) questions not only contribute to clarifying the situation or initial position but also serve as a potential for new, further ideas. Individuals move here in the tension field between "causal understanding" and speculative forecasts (see also Sect. 5.1.3). The greed for "objects of desire" can also have an inspiring effect on creativity when ultimately everything is attempted to obtain them and satisfy personal desires. In auctions or bidding, the sometimes unrestrained "bidding behavior" of interested participants (or participants) may be a good (and impressive) example of this.

Selfish behavioral tendencies or inclinations find their limits when the sought-after personal advantages can only be achieved at the expense of other people, e.g., in manipulative behavior in negotiations or in "fraudulent deception," or at the expense of the general public (or a collective) or the "public purse," such as in tax evasion or in obtaining social benefits fraudulently. Especially in the "shady" borderline areas, such as in tax law or in the declaration of damage cases to insurance companies, imagination or creativity, driven by selfish impulses, finds an unexpected unfolding and often no boundaries or scruples in behavior (see the findings of Webley et al., 2001, on the motivation of tax evasion and Fechtenhauer, 1999, on the influence of selfishness on insurance fraud).

Egoists are not always concerned with material advantages like money or possessions; they often strive for *social prestige* or social recognition or admiration. Thus, their character already takes on narcissistic traits, which are embodied in the guiding principle *"I am the center of the universe!"* But not only the "self-love" or the urge for fame and to be constantly and always admired by others is inherent to narcissists or egoists. They are also masters of manipulation when they "slip into the skin of a Machiavellian" and use and play out their arsenal of manipulation techniques, naturally only for their own advantage or to gain influence and power. What manipulation maneuvers to expect has probably been sufficiently described and discussed in the professional literature (see, e.g., Wienkamp, 2022a, 2023b, in preparation a).

Their role-playing also includes masquerading when they disguise themselves as a chameleon to *not stand out negatively* in critical situations, such as in public (see the experimental results of Bateson et al., 1999, on disguised selfish behavior in public or under observation). In all these situational challenges, versatile, virtuosic behavior is essential, which can only succeed by drawing on creativity potentials.

Sometimes, an altruistic attitude and corresponding behavior, such as pronounced helpfulness, can come under scrutiny if, for example, the helper is suspected of having self-serving motives for their rather *tactical behavior*. According to this view, supposedly selfless motives are also a disguise or masquerade, as they are generally considered irrational and unnatural. Moreover, they would also hide behind or contradict the fundamental interpersonal principle of "give and take," since, in principle, all human interactions—sooner or later—lead to or must lead to a fair balance to achieve harmony in relationships. Altruistic behavior can also serve as a tactical game to soothe one's conscience or to atone for (supposed) guilt.

Egoistic intentions and behavior patterns are indispensable in normal, everyday life and shape social relationships in various (creative) ways. In whatever relationship we find ourselves, these behaviors, which each have their own interests in mind, must always be anticipated.

Be that as it may, there are initially no logical, natural, or contradictory opposites between creativity and egoism that are immediately noticeable and obvious. Rather, it is assumed that self-serving behavioral tendencies or drives stimulate creative thinking to exploit opportunities and realize and secure tangible advantages.

6.4 Small Group Research

For decades, workgroups or teams as "small groups" have attracted attention and research interest regarding their specific problem-solving competence. Group dynamic processes can be beneficial and allow the diverse competencies of team members to be fully and better utilized and developed than individual efforts alone. Working or learning in groups means unlocking, releasing, and utilizing *synergies*. However, teamwork can also prove disadvantageous under certain conditions, for example, if group members do not get along and atmospheric disturbances arise. Then, the group members focus more on themselves and their feelings than on the matter or the actual tasks.

As social psychological research (see, for example, Hofstätter, 1957/1971, pp. 57 ff.) has found, a (small) group always seeks a binding reference norm either through mutual observation or tacitly for behavioral alignment, as demonstrated by earlier "classic experiments" on judgment formation through conformity. In these experiments, participants were willing to revise their originally correct assessments despite knowing better. Out of fear of social isolation, they succumbed to conformity pressure and adapted.

The formation of *"social norms by determination"* not only has scientific-theoretical significance and relevance but also finds application in practice, such as in organizations. For example, in employee evaluations, superiors are often influenced by an assumed or imagined performance norm or other behavioral maxims and tacitly use them as a standard for their employees without ever having provided realistic and substantial evidence for this (see Wienkamp, 2022b).

Groups can also create a noticeable added value with their qualitatively different resources and competencies and, if you will, spur each other on to enormous productivity or creativity and thrive. Evidence of this is the numerous creativity techniques (see, for example, Linneweh, 1984), of which *brainstorming,* based on systematic, successive, and mutual feedback, is probably the best-known and most popular method.

Certain behavioral rules or guidelines, such as the prohibition of evaluating or, even worse, criticizing, devaluing, or rejecting ideas or suggestions from team members during the ongoing process, are conducive to creativity in these techniques. Early evaluations of perhaps absurd, bizarre, or chaotic-seeming ideas bring creativity to an immediate end, as they undermine the spontaneity that is absolutely necessary for the "playful" handling of creative ideas.

Research activities on creative processes are mostly based on behavioral observations, whether directly or indirectly using film or video recordings, which are then analyzed and evaluated by an observer panel. Finally, the results as "products" of a creative process should speak for themselves.

With the method of *"Theme-Centered Interaction (TCI)"* by Ruth Cohn (e.g., 1983), creative problem-solving processes can also be applied to social, interpersonal, or individual problems or conflicts. TCI is based on a triangular relationship between the individual or group member (= I), the group (= WE), and the topic or problem to be addressed (= IT) (see Fig. 6.1 from Wienkamp, 2022b, p. 141).

Through group feedback and the interventions of the group leader via interpretations or interpretations of the group dynamics, that is, the current *"Here and Now,"* the group helps each other with their individual problems and works together through *mutual* feedback, but each in their own way and parallel to the other participants, on personal problems when TCI is offered as an alternative to group therapy. Alternatively, TCI can also be used for learning or self-experience groups that are interested in a common topic, such as a relevant topic or issue of employee leadership, without a personal "history of suffering" being present. Thus, not only individual problems shape the processing process of TCI, but also problems or topics such as leadership issues or questions of collaboration, etc., can be discussed to reach a common understanding or result.

For addressing a factual problem (e.g., a reorganization of a business area or the development of a new strategy for a business field), TCI is also suitable as a forum if the participants do not only attempt to tackle a common problem alone but expect a corresponding know-how input either from the seminar leader or from designated expert speakers. For example, when introducing a new assessment system or when being installed as a leader, an assessment seminar is advisable or mandatory, which ideally should be planned and conducted according to a TCI curriculum (see Wienkamp, 2022b, pp. 141 ff.).

In training personal competence, such as in leadership seminars on "cooperative leadership" or the like, the training of *intuition* should primarily be the focus and considered an essential seminar goal, as it is a crucial prerequisite and foundation for creative behavior! Creativity is required in social processes when it is necessary to deal adequately with defensive attitudes or uncertainties as diffuse fears, in order to neutralize and dissolve resistances or blockages.

Since the TCI methodology has its origins in psychoanalytic group therapy (see, e.g., Grinberg et al., 1971), the group leader should definitely pay attention to the *transference* of past and repressed psychological events or similar and address and bring them up. Transferences are characterized by the following negative developments and effects:

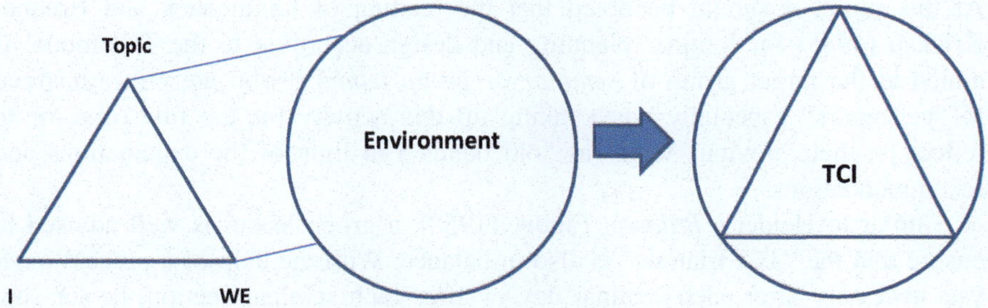

Fig. 6.1 TCI–Triangular Relationship. (From Wienkamp, 2022b, p. 141)

(1) Past experiences are involuntarily *projected* onto the current events—or onto those present in the group—(e.g., when a group participant is chosen as a scapegoat in place of former "tormentors").
(2) Confusions thus lead to *unconscious self-deceptions.*
(3) This leads to *unrealistic* expectations or demands.

How a seminar should be planned and designed according to the TCI model can be derived from the various concepts with different emphases. Without claiming completeness, the specialist literature is based on the following essential considerations and thought processes (cf. Langmaack & Braune-Krickau, 1985):

(a) It is important to consider with what "baggage" of personal experiences the seminar participants arrive and what fantasies may arise from it.
(b) Participants should be met where they are.
(c) The topic (in TCI the IT) is to be understood and presented as a common thematic "bracket"—either with the seminar announcement (title) or in therapy or self-experience groups with the introduction of the group leader.
(d) To "get everyone on board," a brainstorming session at the beginning of the seminar may be necessary (*"What does the topic say to me and what do I know about it?"*) to determine experiential knowledge on the one hand and to design a content structure for processing from this pool on the other.
(e) Rules and principles of communication should be established (e.g., *"Disturbances take precedence"*) and linked with the requirements of metacommunication about the communication process itself.
(f) Both preferences in terms of likes or priorities and *"blind spots"* should be pointed out, and participants should be sensitized to them.
(g) It follows that attention should be drawn to the differences between the factual level (or content level) and the psychosocial level (or emotional level) (ideally, the metaphor would be the "iceberg" with the factual topics as the visible part and the invisible psychosocial part below the water surface).
(h) It is also important to consider when a group structure would be achieved for workability and a group identity (with a sense of belonging).
(i) At the end of the seminar, on the one hand, a content summary of the group or work result should ensure a "transfer assurance" with a regulated transition into practice, and on the other hand, participants must be able to emotionally say goodbye to each other—to "resonate out" and detach from the group.

At this point, it should be noted that the reading of Langmaack and Braune-Krickau (1985) for seminar planning and design according to the TCI model is aimed at the target group of *seminar or group leaders*, who are either inspired to "get smart," especially when taking up this activity for the first time, or to reflect on their previous work (as "old hands") in light of the explanations and recommendations.

Similar to Heider's *Balance Theory* (1958), a group leader is well advised to ensure that the "TCI triangle" is also in balance. With the help of a process analysis necessary after each seminar day or after each seminar section, he (or she) should ask whether one of the three TCI components is overshadowing the others, e.g., if the group as WE increasingly focuses on itself at the expense of the topic (as IT), or if individual participants (as I) push themselves to the forefront or, conversely, do not participate at all. It would also be helpful for the seminar leader to create a sociogram of the group after the individual phases, recording who in the group has become very close and is forming coalitions, who is feeling alienated, and which seminar attendees have already clashed and are beginning to resolve their personal conflicts. The seminar leader should also locate themselves in the sociogram and finally plan the further "dramaturgy" or the next steps or interventions.

At the latest during the final discussion of the seminar event, there may be another opportunity for creativity diagnostics. Because the participants each share their impressions from the seminar with the plenary, drawing only their *personal conclusion* from their individual perspective. With the contributions of the other group members, they should recognize what remained hidden from them and what they simply "did not have on their radar," i.e., forgot. By collectively compiling all individual conclusions, a complete picture emerges for each attendee through this *creative* feedback process, which can be considered a creative advancement.

A seminar according to the TCI method should be the seed that then flourishes creatively through the transfer into practice.

To some extent as a side aspect, social psychological research on the "intergroup level" addressed the so-called *social creativity* as a process to promote self-assertion and maintain equality between different groups. This would be relevant, for example, for students of different disciplines or in the workplace for various professional groups, such as, on the one hand, engineers who are particularly interested in technical perfection, and on the other hand, merchants who are responsible for marketing and the economic benefit or profit derived from it (according to Mummendey & Schreiber, 1984; cited in Spears & Tausch, 2014, p. 537). Psychologically, the two groups make use of a trick as "social creativity" by choosing the characteristic in which they are strong and better, such as engineers in handling technology, and positively measuring and comparing themselves with the other group, being aware of the compensatory effect in collaboration through their respective strengths.

6.5 Summary

Much has been written about the "social world" and its diverse relationships and interactions in the previous two chapters. This chapter focused on topics of social psychology that dealt very intensively with the motivation of individuals in social situations or settings. In addition to achievement motivation and power ambitions, attachment motivation was also part of the relevant model, which can build an important bridge through communication and establish a connection to creativity. Only when people engage with each other and form relationships are the prerequisites for mutual assistance as well as creative and cooperative action given.

Creativity can also be used excellently and virtuously to fulfill self-interests. To achieve important personal goals, many people become very inventive and, if you will, creative in their behavior.

Both work or organizational psychology and other branches of psychology, such as "clinical psychology" with its group therapeutic procedures, have embraced the insights into group dynamics or the so-called small group research. From this, as a derivation from psychoanalytic group therapy, "theme-centered interaction," or TCI for short, has emerged and been created. It is a preferred methodology to address and work on both factual problems and problems of personality development within a group. As already emphasized in an earlier model, the balance theory, it is also important in this method that the components I, WE, and IT (for the topic) are in a dynamic balance, and the group or seminar leader is responsible for this with their process analyses and interventions.

Between different groups, it does not necessarily have to lead to ruinous competitive relationships, but more prosperous forms on the "intergroup level" are also possible, such as the handling of "social creativity" for mutual benefit.

7 Creativity Diagnostics Within the Framework of Personality Assessment

For a general or comprehensive psychodiagnostics, a whole range of concepts with many methodological implementation paths or variants is fundamentally available (see also Chap. 4). Exploratory interviews with or without a structured questionnaire, e.g., for anamnesis in clinical psychology or for conducting applicant interviews, as well as personality tests or methods of behavioral observation, such as in an assessment center (AC), belong to this "toolbox."

When using personality tests, the course of exploration or the diagnostic examination is predetermined, i.e., standardized, to ensure the objectivity of the diagnostic procedure. By means of norms, e.g., according to age groups, gender, or education, it is possible to convert the raw test scores into the norm values representative of the population group, e.g., as a percentile rank or stanine value, and to make a qualified assessment, primarily to conduct *interindividual comparisons*. Percentile ranks assign the available test results to a comparison group from 100% to 1% according to their "best placement," so that a percentile rank of, for example, 70% indicates that 30% of the tested individuals in the comparison group achieved a better test performance. When applying the stanine classification, the test results are assigned to *nine* performance categories, with this standardized scale defining that no values are greater than 9 and less than 1. If the tests are reliable and valid, the interpretation of the test findings is also serious and meaningful and can be used for practical decisions. On this basis, for example, a specific statement (with "yes" or "no") is allowed, such as the hiring of an examined applicant or to make a most likely accurate diagnosis that indicates corresponding therapeutic measures.

Which tests are applied is usually a factual decision of the responsible test user and depends both on the *target group,* such as school children, mentally ill individuals, or job applicants, and on the *diagnostic purpose,* i.e., whether a selection decision is pending or whether a specific support measure or other measure for behavior modification is to be considered, which is to be clarified or decided with the test result.

H. Wienkamp, *Creativity Diagnostics*, https://doi.org/10.1007/978-3-662-70432-5_7

Of course, most practitioners in psychological diagnostics are likely to know the "classics" of personality tests, such as the *"Minnesota Multiphasic Personality Inventory (MMPI)"* by Hathaway (originally 1947; cited after Hathaway & McKinley, 1943/1951) in the psychiatric field, which, for example, Eysenck (1970) used as a precursor and reference test with his tests (e.g., the *"Eysenck Personality Scale"* or *EPS* or also called *EPQ*, see Eysenck & Eysenck, 1991). Based on Eysenck's tests, the now very popular *"Big Five"* (see e.g., Costa & McCrae, 1992) as well as the *"HEXACO"* by Lee and Ashton (2004) as a personality test with the additional *sixth* trait scale "*honesty* and *humility*" are based.

Other psychometric personality procedures, such as the *"Behavioral Inhibition Systems and Behavioral Approach (or Activation) Systems (BIV/BAS scales)"* by Carver and White (1994), are based on differing personality models, such as the *"Reinforcement Sensitivity Theory (RST)"* by Gray (1971, 1987; Gray & McNaughton, 2000), which focus more on goal- or preference-oriented behavior with approach and avoidance tendencies. Their orientation and construction naturally follow their own personality traits, such as reward sensitivity and the avoidance of anxiety or conflict situations (see also Wienkamp, 2017, 2020a, for details).

Finally, there are self-descriptions or self-assessments of one's own (assumed) creativity as personality procedures. Such instruments may seem unusual and daring in terms of validity at first glance, considering the general problem of *"social desirability"* in test applications, which has already led to the failure of a number of validation studies in the past. Nevertheless, the attempt is worthwhile in terms of further personality and creativity research, as in the ideal case, a connection between personal creativity assessment and defined personality traits could be established and demonstrated alongside objective creativity performances. However, this presupposes that creative behavior and the self-assessment of creativity are highly correlated.

Normally, neither clinical nor more "commercial" personality tests contain direct references or connections to creativity, as creativity in personality research is classified and treated more as a cognitive performance or behavior, and on the other hand, as already mentioned several times, it is difficult to operationalize and measure in a test situation. However, it cannot be ruled out that the question of creative potential arises within a personality diagnosis, for example, to assess the available resources or resilience (resistance or elasticity), for example, in dealing with "critical life events" and overcoming them (e.g., through effective coping), and to make a statement about it. Given the multitude of personality constructs and diagnostic questions, the interest was to distinguish creativity from other cognitive performances such as intelligence or problem-solving ability within the framework of a differential diagnosis and to determine it.

Therefore, it made sense to examine and discuss the classic personality tests as well as other test concepts for possible connections to a person's creativity. In contrast to the explanations in Chap. 4, the focus is now less on a general description and discussion of the feature complexes or personality traits associated with creativity, but rather on the instruments or feature scales developed for this purpose and available on the market with their specific feature facets or aspects, to enable a personality diagnosis.

7.1 The "Classics" of Personality Tests and Their Possible Relation to Creativity

As a pronounced "classic" of personality tests, the test versions of Eysenck and Eysenck (1991) are considered precursors for subsequent developments, as well as the now very popular "Big Five" personality constructs by Costa and McCrae (1992) or McCrae and Costa (1999).

7.1.1 The Feature Scales of Eysenck

In the EPS by Eysenck and Eysenck (1991), which is based on a series of precursors as a personality test and therefore belongs without reservation to the "classics" mentioned here, the feature dimension *Extraversion–Introversion* and perhaps also *Neuroticism* are rather unlikely to be associated with creativity, although some authors attest that both extraverted and *non*-neurotic, i.e., emotionally stable, individuals find it easier to engage in creative behavior.

However, with the feature *Psychoticism*, there is a suspicion that creativity or even "genius" sometimes corresponds with madness or other "psychological peculiarities or exaggerations." Poets, for example, are said to have emotional disturbances that not only contribute to a higher suicide rate but also "influence them to create brilliant works" (Baudson, 2011). In light of the assumption that "genius and madness" are closely linked, Barron (1965, p. 47 ff.) also pointed out that creative individuals often stand out as "eccentrics" and receive much attention, but due to their *ego strength* (see also Sect. 4.4), they distinguish themselves from psychiatric syndromes, so that psychopathological disorders did not occur excessively often in this population group. According to the studies at that time, the feature "ego strength" even correlated negatively with diseases from the psychiatric spectrum. Kaufman (2022, p. 83 ff.) pointed out, in light of current research, both the negative connections between creativity and "mental disorders" and the positive influences that creativity can offer to mental health and particularly to strengthening resilience as willpower and resistance, and considers it idle, if not even dangerous, to speculate about the (supposed) liaison between creativity and madness given the current state of knowledge.

As far as is known, the feature *Psychoticism* by Eysenck (1977) was not designed in this way, but it is associated with deviant (antisocial or problematic) attitudes and behavior and rather addresses problem cases from the psychopathological or criminal milieu, which fundamentally have little to do with creativity in the actual and positive sense.

Ruch (1999), who transformed and validated the EPQ by Eysenck into a German-language version, found that the items of the parallel existing and accompanying lie scale partially overlapped with the items of the psychoticism scale when they loaded on a common factor or had a high loading when applying factor analysis. This result is plausible and understandable in content, as criminals or other socio- or psychopaths have no scruples about lying! In this sense, neither psychoticism nor a willingness to lie has anything in common with creativity.

7.1.2 The Personality Traits of the "Big Five"

In addition to the trait (1) "Openness to New Experiences," which is of particular interest here in connection with creativity, the Big Five also includes the personality dispositions (2) "Extraversion–Introversion," (3) "Neuroticism," (4) "Agreeableness," and (5) "Conscientiousness."

Rammstedt and John (2005) developed both a significantly shortened standard version compared to earlier versions and adaptations for the German-speaking area, the *"Big Five Inventory (BFI),"* as well as a short version of the Big Five, namely the *"BFI-K"* with only 21 items (instead of 44 items). The trait scale *"Openness to New Experiences"*, which is of interest regarding creativity diagnostics, achieved slightly poorer reliability measures (Cronbach's Alpha as internal consistency) in the short version compared to the longer test version, which is not surprising given the brevity of the test; however, the test scores were sufficiently stable or consistent and were still in a tolerable range at slightly below $r = 0.70$. In the subsequent correlation analysis, this trait was relatively clearly distinguished from the other personality dispositions and emphasized its independence. A separate factor with relatively high loadings of the associated items could also be demonstrated for the trait "Openness to New Experiences." The content of the items in this trait scale included the attitude towards art and aesthetics *("Appreciate artistic and aesthetic experiences")* and the extent of interest and imagination *("Am interested in many things"; "Am deep, like to think about things").*

However, the test authors refrained from relating the Big Five traits to creative achievements or behavior and, for example, from calculating and reporting correlation coefficients as a measure of relationship. Thus, there is no evidence that this test construction of the personality trait "Openness to New Experiences" is directly correlated with creativity.

As expected, the studies cited by some textbook authors (e.g., Schuler & Görlich, 2007) and previous studies suggested that openness to new experiences—as well as *curiosity* and *intrinsic motivation* as related or similar personality dispositions for creative achievements and behavior—is beneficial and could be positively associated with this trait (see also Sect. 3.1).

7.2 Personality Tests Based on Goal- and Interest-Driven Approach and Avoidance Behavior

Starting with the moral philosophy of Jeremy Bentham (1780/1823), who reduced life in nature as well as humanity and its civilization to the experiences of *"Pleasure & Pain,"* thus seeing a "natural law" as the source of action, science dedicated itself to the principles of action in connection with personal preferences. Later, the two brothers James and John Stuart Mill (see e.g., Dickinson, 1924) expanded this principle of action by combining all learning processes of living beings with this experience of pleasure and pain, or in the training of animals through the use of rewards and punishments, and made it a mandatory prerequisite.

Many decades later, approach and avoidance behavior appeared in various contexts, particularly in "learning or behaviorist psychology," as learning processes that are also based on reinforcement mechanisms such as rewarding or punishing (or their conscious avoidance as negative reinforcement) in learning theory.

7.2.1 The "Approach and Avoidance Temperament Questionnaire (ATQ)"

At the operational level, this led to test constructions or the development of questionnaires that were used as instruments in personality research. With the *"Approach and Avoidance Temperament Questionnaire (ATQ)"*, Elliot and Thrash (2008, p. 333) operationalized approach or avoidance tendencies using a relatively short questionnaire of six items each on a seven-point scale as self-assessment. Avoidance behavior, for example, is addressed by *Item 1* with the formulation:

> "By nature, I am a very nervous person."

Approach behavior is expressed, for example, by *Item 2*:

> "Thinking about the things I want really energizes me"

Their validity studies (Elliot & Thrash, 2002) used the Big Five traits as indicators to examine the influence of these two fundamental behavioral tendencies on achievement motivation (e.g., for a successful exam). With the subsequent path or structural analysis, they confirmed the model of these two factors and recommended generally examining the variables of a personality theory additionally for these fundamental, but intermediate and latent influencing factors.

7.2.2 "Promotion Focus" and "Prevention Focus"

Similarly, Higgins (1997) also proposed a motivational model with approach and avoidance behavior and referred to these motivational systems as "Promotion Focus" and "Prevention Focus." According to his findings, it is characteristic that individuals use both systems interchangeably, but according to their nature, they use one of these systems more frequently. An instrument was constructed by Lockwood et al. (2002) also for self-assessment with the *"Promotion/Prevention Scales"* with *nine* items each and a scale from *1* to *9*. Promotion Focus was operationalized, for example, by an item like:

"Overall, I am more oriented toward achieving success than preventing failure."

Prevention Focus was presented, for example, by the following item:

"I am anxious that I will fail short of my responsibilities and obligations."

Promotion Focus was dominant in the studies when "role models" set positive goals that were emulated. Prevention Focus, on the other hand, was considered an avoidance strategy to circumvent or avoid unpleasant experiences.

7.2.3 The "BIS and BAS Scales"

Carver and White (1994) developed the *"Behavioral Inhibition Scale"* and the *"Behavioral Approach Scale,"* in short, the "BIS/BAS Scales," based on the "Reinforcement Sensitivity Theory (RST)" as a test procedure, which is also available in a German version by Strobel et al. (2001). The feature structure applies to both the English and the German version:

a) BIS total scale for sensitivity to anxiety and conflicts;
Exemplary item: "When I think something unpleasant is going to happen, I usually feel pretty uneasy."
b) BAS Drive scale for drive and determination;
Exemplary item: "I go out of my way to get what I want."
c) BAS Reward Responsiveness scale for sensitivity to joy and success;
Exemplary item: "When something good happens to me, it affects me strongly."
d) BAS Fun Seeking scale for the search for fun and desire for new experiences;
Exemplary item: "I am always willing to try something new if I think it will be fun."

Since the test developers of the German version could not confirm the four-factor structure in their empirical study, they advocated for a simple and straightforward *two-factor* (possibly also three-factor) solution and combined the three BAS scales into a BAS total scale alongside the BIS scale.

Contrary to this result with the German version, other researchers (see, for example, Caseras et al., 2003) have examined the BIS/BAS scales and often found a multi-factor structure that varied from study to study. Caseras et al. (2003)

extracted, for example, in addition to a BIS factor, three BAS sub-factors, which they named based on the item assignments as follows:

a) Impulsiveness-thrill seeking (in German: Impulsivität und Nervenkitzel)
b) Extraversion (with a focus or emphasis on sociability)
c) Reward interested (in German: Anreiz- und Belohnungssensibilität)

Of course, this test instrument with the BIS/BAS scales (like the previously presented instruments or scales of Sect. 7.2) was not yet related to creative behavior, so no correlation measures are available so far.

In summary, the structural solutions or offerings for the RST and thus for the associated feature scales like the BIS and BAS scales are inconsistent, partly contradictory, and therefore not yet satisfactory (see also the individual contributions in the anthology by Corr, 2008).

7.2.4 Incentive Motivation and Other Personality Traits as Possible Correlates to Creativity

In view of this predicament with the scale constructions against the background of the RST, Wienkamp (2017) redesigned these feature constructs in his dissertation according to his research hypotheses and, for example, followed Andresen (e.g., 2000) in his opinion on risk behavior, that for the BIS, a bifactorial structure likely exists with both a drive factor such as *impulsivity, risk-taking, sensation seeking* or even (exaggerated or inappropriate) *recklessness* on one hand, and an opposing anxiety factor representing *conflict avoidance, risk aversion* and *caution* on the other hand. In contrast to this view, according to RST, impulsivity embodies the BAS trait complex and is understood as a counterpart or antagonist to the BIS as the seat of anxiety!

For the BAS area, on the other hand, feature variables and alternative constructs were sought and chosen that enter into a substantive connection with selfish behavioral tendencies or self-interest and were termed as *incentive motivation* (or *"incentive motivation"* in the sense of Hull, 1943, 1951). In this study, the personality traits *egoism, greed* and *Machiavellianism* correlated as expected with incentive motivation, which was constructed as an independent trait scale, and had a significant influence on risky decisions (also called risk decisions) through a latent or overarching incentive and reward factor, which were operationalized as decision scenarios with alternative preferences for incentives and risks. Incidentally, incentive motivation would very strongly align with the subfactor by Caseras et al. (2003), *"Reward interested,"* and largely correspond to it.

That self-interests may possibly be compatible with the occurrence of creativity and might even be a "driver" for creative achievements and behavior was already touched upon and discussed in Sect. 6.3.

For creativity studies, features such as *incentive motivation* and *risk tolerance* from the test for *diagnostics of an economic and financial personality,* the *"Six*

& Six" (Wienkamp, in preparation b), could be used within the framework of a more comprehensive personality diagnostics from the area of approach or avoidance behavior (or the BIS or BAS area). These two test scales sufficiently cover approach and avoidance behavior in the form of their available test items. For example, an item for incentive motivation reads:

> "When conducting a business, I always have to think about the next business."

And for risk tolerance, an item chosen was, for example:

> "I like to make bets with myself about whether a future event will occur or a prophecy will come true or not."

To measure risk-taking, the risk scale in the *"Hamburg Personality Inventory (HPI)"* by Andresen (2002) is suitable, as well as for *"sensation seeking"* the trait scale by Gniech et al. (1993), which is widespread in the German-speaking area and has been used in many studies.

For an assessment of self-confidence or self-esteem or the like, which are beneficial as accompanying and influencing personality dispositions for creativity (see Sect. 3.2), the German-language scale originally by Rosenberg was offered (Collani & Herzberg, 2003).

From the personality test *"Six & Six"* with its feature structure for both a core area and an outer area of personality, which primarily depict "business requirements (see Fig. 7.1), another interesting feature scale would be the personality

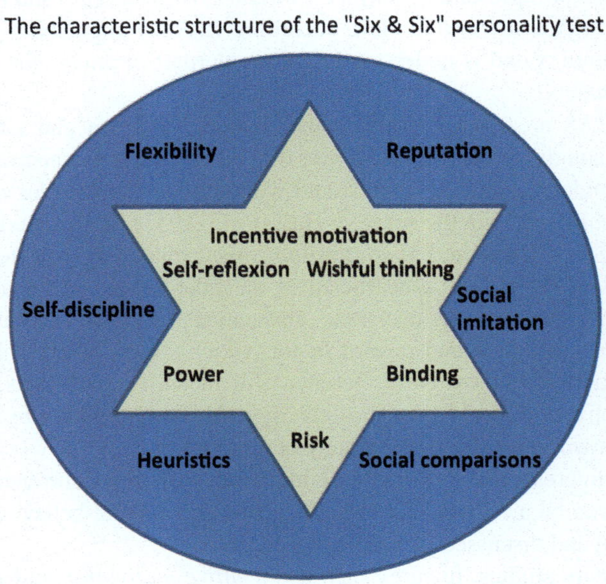

Fig. 7.1 Feature structure of the personality test Six & Six (Wienkamp, in preparation b)

disposition *"heuristics"*, which could most likely be associated with creative behavior. An item of this feature variable would read, for example:

> "When managing my financial investments, I always have the result of the last business as a 'benchmark' or guideline involuntarily in mind."

For other personality constructs such as *flexibility* (as included in other tests and also in Six & Six) and *wishful thinking* as a sign of "healthy vs. exaggerated optimism" with the poles *realistic* vs. *illusory* (also in *Six & Six*), it is conceivable and not to be excluded that they also correlate with creativity.

7.3 Other Personality Procedures for Self-Assessment of Creativity

Under the title *Creativity Assessment*, the authors Qian et al. (2022, pp. 229 ff.) presented various instruments for creativity assessment, primarily for self-assessment, which have appeared exclusively in the USA or the English-speaking world until recently. These creativity tests, based on self-assessments, clearly and decisively differentiate themselves from the test procedures or trait scales published and used in German, which are or were related to creativity or probably covary with this construct and whose trait expression is either conducive to creativity or inhibits or blocks its occurrence.

A certainly controversial procedure in the past was self-assessments of one's own creativity or creative achievements (products) in certain areas, such as with the *"Creative Behavior Inventory (CBI)"* by Hocevar (1979; cited in Qian et al., 2022, p. 233). This creativity test attempted to capture and compare the (possible) creativity in given "domains" such as literature, music, art, etc., through self-assessment, using a frequency indication combined with the statement or evaluation: *the more frequent, the more creative*.

In parallel, another procedure, the *"Creative Achievement Questionnaire (CAQ)"* by Carson et al. (2005; cited in Qian et al., 2022, pp. 233 f.), aimed to achieve a self-assessment of a previously reached standard or quality level in defined domains such as music, for example, whether the person in question only moderately masters a musical instrument or has already given public concerts. This assessment was weighted considering the frequency, for example, if "n" concerts have been given so far, and displayed as a scale value according to a specific procedure.

With the *"Creative Personality Scale (CPS)"* by Gough (1979; cited in Qian et al., 2022, pp. 235 f.), *18 positive* statements and *12 negative* statements (items) on creativity were available, which the test subjects also used for self-assessment. For a positive mention, the test subjects received a point credited, for a negative indication, there was a minus point, which reduced the overall scale value. The *"Short Scale of Creative"* by Karwoski (2014; cited in Qian et al., 2022, p. 236) functions similarly, where *11 items* are to be assessed on a 5-point scale, to what extent they apply to the test person (e.g., *"I think I am a creative person"*).

Whether valid test results can be expected with the help of these self-assessments remains to be seen. The contribution of the authors does not contain any information on this. Problems of "social desirability" as well as simply misjudgments of the test subjects cannot generally be ruled out in a normal test application. It is not or is difficult to assess at this point whether self-assessments could possibly complement and enrich creativity and personality diagnostics or whether they are entirely out of place!

At most, self-assessments, for whatever diagnostic purpose, are useful if, for example, in the case of demonstrably creative vs. non-creative individuals, extreme group comparisons are used within the framework of a *"backward or reverse strategy"* to find the items with discrimination potential that best differentiate between these groups.

7.4 Summary

As a summary of this chapter, it was initially suggested to compile the test procedures presented and discussed in the preceding sections, with their many different personality traits, in the form of a synopsis (see Table 7.1) with a view to creativity diagnostics. It is easy to see that this is a recipe, or at least an offer, with which personality constructs or trait scales from existing personality tests can be used to calculate measures of association (e.g., correlations) with observable creative performances.

Table 7.1 Synopsis of the operationalized traits in various personality tests

Trait	Operationalization and Measurement
Creativity	+ Observation of creative behavior + Creativity tests + Self-descriptions for creativity assessment
Personality traits associated with creativity ***§ Openness to new experiences*** §§ Curiosity §§ Intrinsic motivation ***§ Approach/Avoidance behavior*** §§ BIS/BAS system §§ Incentive motivation §§ Risk tolerance §§ Sensation seeking ***§ Self-confidence/Self-esteem*** ***§ Heuristics***	e.g., "BFI" by Rammstedt & John (2005) e.g., "ATQ" by Elliot & Thrash (2008) e.g., "Promotion/Prevention Scales" by Lockwood et al. (2002) e.g., "BIS/BAS Scales" by Strobel et al. (2001) e.g., "Incentive Motivation" and "Risk Tolerance" from the "Six & Six" by Wienkamp (in preparation b) e.g., the risk scale of the HPI (Andresen, 2002) e.g., "Sensation Seeking" by Gniech et al. (1993) e.g., scale for self-esteem (Collani & Herzberg, 2003) e.g., "Heuristic" from the "Six & Six" by Wienkamp (in preparation b)

Certainly, there are many alternatives to this selection of scales and instruments for the mentioned trait complexes, which address and thematize motivational and cognitive behavior. At least when it comes to English-language procedures for personality diagnostics, the instruments listed in Table 7.1 would additionally be suitable for this.

The selection of trait areas or trait complexes (see Chap. 3) is unlikely to change much, as they are very likely associated with creativity.

8 Take Aways

In conclusion, the most important insights about creativity and its diagnostics are summarized once more and condensed into pointed statements. This is connected with the purpose and goal of appreciating or reflecting on the previously discussed explanations from a greater distance and from another concluding and retrospective perspective, and deriving general theses or statements from them that hopefully provide sufficient orientation.

8.1 Creativity—A Challenging Terrain to Navigate

Many researchers have "cut their teeth" on the topic of creativity or creativity diagnostics. While creativity as a personality trait essentially depends on the correct understanding and an appropriate and accurate definition for the respective field, creativity diagnostics also involves the problem of determination and measurement under controlled and comparable conditions. Many creativity researchers have discussed and treated creativity under the *"4 P's"*, that is, under the aspects of: *Person, Product, Process* and (in English) *Press,* to get closer to creativity as a construct. A simplified and equally helpful pragmatic and practical assumption and definition is: *Creativity must produce something new and useful and convince the people affected by it.*

Apart from intelligence, which always appears in connection with creativity and is rightly emphasized due to its undeniable influence on creative performance and behavior, creativity tends to be understood more as an *independent* trait or construct that, like many other personality traits, must assert itself in a *"nosological network"* of related or similar psychological traits and is subject to their influences as well as influencing them itself. Especially in solving still open problems, creativity, just like intelligence, is required and demanded as a basic prerequisite to solve them. Of course, other personality dispositions also influence these

H. Wienkamp, *Creativity Diagnostics*, https://doi.org/10.1007/978-3-662-70432-5_8

problem-solving processes, for example, when concentration, perseverance, or even courage and willingness to take risks are needed.

Most creativity researchers agree that creativity is not something involuntary or mystical and does not "fall from the sky," but always builds on existing old or basic knowledge and must be *connectable* in the professional domain if something new is to emerge that significantly improves the status quo.

8.2 If You Want to Understand Creativity, You Should also Keep Intelligence in Mind

Due to the correlative relationships between several intelligence factors and creativity, it can be assumed that the emergence of creative achievements involves one or another intellectual talent or performance, or even a whole bundle of these mental abilities. In addition to correlation analyses, factor analyses, in particular, help to specifically determine common causative or background (latent) influencing factors that are closely related to these mental abilities and exert a common influence on any intellectual or creative performance. Another question is then, from which intelligence model and from which components of intelligence, whether from "divergent thinking" or "convergent thinking" or "inductive thinking" vs. "deductive thinking," etc., one should start.

However, not to be forgotten are the so-called *metacognitions,* which are responsible as overarching psychological mechanisms for the success of many intelligent solution processes and attempts and therefore have many similarities to creativity. The same situation fundamentally applies to other psychological mechanisms, such as the *"emotional memory"* as a repository of intuition or "intuitive intelligence" to support (difficult) decisions and to navigate uncertain and opaque situations, as well as the use of *heuristics,* which are very similar in their handling to creativity and are often confused with it due to their assumed problem-solving potential. Heuristics, due to their hedonistic influence, are no guarantee of being correct in judgments!

Otherwise, intelligence research knows two fundamentally different research approaches, namely "bottom-up" and "top-down," which lead to the determination and identification of intelligence performances based on different concepts. In the *top-down design,* the starting point is the general factor of intelligence, from which the known sub-factors such as reading comprehension or verbal fluency are to be derived factually-logically and in accordance with theory. Conversely, the *bottom-up approach* takes the empirically provided performances (on the tasks or items) in the intelligence test as a total performance and extracts from them so-called main components as intelligence factors for specific mental abilities such as memory performance, numerical understanding, vocabulary, etc. In this evaluation method, the variability in the processed tasks of the intelligence test is to be bundled by identifying common (latent) influencing factors, thereby explaining part of the variance (or dispersion) in the performance results. Other classifications and representations are also possible, such as the division according to linguistic vs. scientific or technical talent and performance capability.

All in all, intellectual activity boils down to recognizing (hidden) rules or regularities and their *transformation* into new practical applications ("if-then cases") or conversely to abstraction performances, by inductively concluding from individual observations to the abstract overarching totality and deriving and defining structures or systems from it. In addition, there are intelligence concepts of knowledge acquisition (e.g., vocabulary learning) and knowledge building through new insights and experiences. Finally, the more intellectual models of thinking or the use of cognitive abilities must be distinguished from the rather operational and process-oriented models (see also Sect. 8.4).

Intelligence tests by no means replace creativity diagnostics, as creativity is and remains an independent cognitive achievement.

8.3 Creativity is More Than Just a "Catchphrase"!

If creativity is not synonymous with intelligence or, in a narrower sense, problem-solving ability, then what is this trait? This is likely the question when discussing creativity as a concept or personality disposition!

As has already become clear, overlaps or parallels with intelligence research or intelligence diagnostics cannot be dismissed. Creativity is also not just a "glittering term" or the like. It is undeniable, however, that creativity exerts an enormous fascination and attraction on many people, especially for their commercial lives, like a magnet, which no one can easily resist.

Apart from the dazzling and indescribable aura that clings to creativity and causes it, it would be a mistake or misunderstanding to focus solely on the phenomenon of "creativity" and to leave out the entire network of other personality traits. According to contributions from creativity and personality research, other personality variables also seem to covary with the trait of creativity, such as curiosity and self-confidence, in addition to intelligence. For this reason, it is important to transform creativity into a model and to provide this construct with a "theoretical framework" in order to empirically-statistically investigate and clarify the relationships in the network of different but relevant personality traits. Aspects such as a process logic accompanying creativity or different manifestations of creativity, such as "small" or "big leaps," apostrophized and introduced as "Mini-C's" and "Big-C's," should be considered and discussed in this context.

Qualitatively, creativity can be spoken of when, as already indicated, the ideas or their output are new and useful and receive positive social resonance, which diametrically distinguishes creativity from (new) fantasies, crazy notions, or "sheer nonsense." Metaphors from Gestalt psychology most impressively capture what constitutes and describes creativity, namely the "modeling of a figure on an existing background," which gives the (new) image "a face"—that is more than the sum of its parts. Like a puzzle, it is sometimes necessary to think "outside the box" to get one step closer to the solution. Both childlike curiosity and naive ideas can prove helpful in this creative process in the function of a "catalyst" and help new ideas break through via spontaneous flashes of inspiration or leaps of thought. Rigid mindsets such as prejudices or stereotypes or conformity pressure from outside are detrimental to creativity and certainly anything but conducive.

For creativity research, the differentiation between creativity on the one hand and innovation capability on the other is still relevant. Creativity, as mentioned several times, is related to the ingenuity of new thoughts or ideas as well as a productive linking of prior knowledge with new insights through a skillful combination and decoding of the available information. Innovation capability, on the other hand, involves new ideas or inventions from research being picked up by other people as "managers" and successfully implemented, for example, as "prototypes." Feasibility thinking, reality checks, and project management, where planning and organization are crucial, are the qualities that rightly characterize and distinguish "innovators" as managers.

It would be even better if the new ideas generated in many places or workplaces were collected by a "strategic innovation management" and stored as "company know-how" and continuously updated, so that these new ideas are available as expert knowledge at the appropriate time. Strategic innovation management is not solely dependent on the chosen management philosophy or its conception, such as change management, lean management, or business reengineering, but particularly on the development of IT technology with its diverse application systems.

8.4 Creativity Diagnostics: An "Impossible Task"—Or Possible After All?

Given the multitude of unresolved but previously accepted "handicaps" in creativity diagnostics, it is difficult to propose a coherent and practical diagnostic design. Considering the fact that creativity does not readily manifest itself or cannot be prescribed, previous diagnostic efforts, such as creativity tests, have reached their limits.

Creativity diagnostics cannot be blamed for not having tried *everything* (?) to approach the problem of diagnostics or creativity assessment and to "crack" it methodically. As long as we stick to the diverse research approaches, it seems that, on the one hand, creativity diagnostics is definitely *"domain-dependent"*. Apparently, there is a significant difference between admiring the genius of an artist or scientist and deriving the due creativity from their works and rightly attributing it to the person as an extraordinary talent, or whether it concerns "the man or woman on the street," who are relatively inconspicuous in terms of creativity in comparison. Secondly, the problems of creativity diagnostics lie in the methodology itself, regardless of which target group, such as preschool or school children or adults, for example, in personnel selection and occupational aptitude diagnostics, is to undergo a creativity examination.

Open problems, for which creative ideas are needed, evade a standard and controlled process in examination situations, as the individuals being examined handle them unpredictably and thwart interpersonal comparability, which is obviously not possible and thus omitted. Time pressure or stress almost prevents a relaxed and creative approach to open problems, so it is not surprising that many test-takers cannot think of anything sensible and spontaneity falls by the wayside. Without ideas or (spontaneous) inspirations, there is also no cognitive processing of the information, in whatever mental or intellectual manner, and there are no good problem solutions that fulfill the attribute "creative," meaning new, useful, and accepted by others.

Unfortunately, the use of creativity tests, with the exception of projective tests (such as "fantasy tests"), presupposes standardized and comparable test conditions. Thus, it is no wonder that attempts with tests either failed or the test results led to problems in explanation and interpretation. Such procedural problems of the instruments frequently appeared during their testing and validation, so it was almost a miracle that test constructions and their use in practice occurred at all.

Abundance of ideas for quantity and *diversity of ideas* for variety are, alongside the criteria of *originality* in the sense of rarity and *elaboration* in the sense of developing or "embellishing," the most common and widely used assessment criteria in creativity tests. To make it easier for test users, the test constructors provided evaluation grids, lists of possible ideas, or examples, etc., in the manuals for test evaluation.

Creativity tests in occupational aptitude diagnostics took advantage of experiences from school pedagogy and adopted a number of test tasks for their practical use, such as the number of possible uses for concrete objects, which stimulated imagination and visualization. However, in occupational aptitude diagnostics, a *psychological requirement analysis* should definitely precede the creativity assessment to get an idea of what type of creativity is required at which workplaces and how the expression of creativity can be recognized and evaluated in aptitude diagnostic examinations if necessary.—In practice, managers usually do not have these problems of creativity assessment and evaluation, as they see and experience their employees daily and must also accept and appreciate their "creative" performances as such.

As an alternative to creativity diagnostics based on individual given problems or tasks, test developers attempted a procedural orientation and application by observing and examining the creativity potential from problem recognition to problem-solving or implementation according to *process steps* and embedding it in a so-called cover story if necessary. However, process-related creativity tests have not yet fully met the expectations placed on them in the diagnostics of creative performance and behavior.

In interview questions and case studies, which were sometimes also used to determine creativity potential, creativity diagnostics largely depend on the use of suitable assessment systems that, similar to process design, evaluate creative approaches in a graduated manner based on a given grid and allow for differentiated judgments. It might also be helpful, under certain circumstances, not only to look *directly* at creativity but to design and collect a *profile of characteristics* within the framework of an *indirect* diagnosis to capture the network of personality traits that are associated with creative behavior and either demonstrably promote or block it (see also Sect. 8.7). Further information and insights can also be contributed in applicant interviews by biographical questions and their answers regarding creative activities such as hobbies, interests, etc.

8.5 Creativity in the "Social World"

After the material world, where creations prove to be products or similar, creativity in the "social world" is dedicated to interpersonal relationships, both with a positive side, as in romantic love relationships, and with a negative tinge in human problems or social conflicts. The medium here is verbal communication with the (speech) contributions of the communicating persons, which can sometimes be "creative" in the sense of being novel or surprising. Rigid attitudes such as prejudices or clichés, on the other hand, prevent original or creative contributions and push communication into the usual familiar paths without noticeable progress for the relationship. Imaginations or distorted images of reality are not excluded. Instead, it would be better and more helpful to listen to one's or another's feelings in social situations with other people and take the emotions seriously.

On the basis of "social constructions," which are nothing more than a multiple information processing from perception to evaluation of the ongoing social process, every social being explores the perceived events and finds their social understanding. The (own) self is always involved in this, so that due to self-assessments, it sometimes leads to false conclusions or misunderstandings in communication, especially when the model of the *"cognitive miser"* (English: cognitive miser) is active out of sheer convenience and simply attributes prematurely, for example, by blaming the character or incompetence of another person for everything negative. Situational influences as well as coincidences are gladly overlooked or simply ignored as explanations or excuses for the unfavorable behavior of other people. Quick or hasty judgments are particularly likely when the events that have occurred do not meet expectations, and out of sheer uncertainty, either simple explanations are sought, or reinterpretations or devaluations take place, for example, of other people who hold a different opinion, so that one's own worldview is restored and the individual finds their peace of mind.

In disturbed social relationships with a lot of conflict potential, creativity unfortunately shows its "dark" or negative side and acts destructively on the relationship, at the expense of harmony and stability.

Much depends on creativity in social situations on one's own judgment or category systems, which were acquired and built up in the course of personality development. They serve to pack social events or unfamiliar people into the appropriate "drawer." Sometimes or for many people, "implicit personality theories" can arise from this, which then become stereotypes and disturb the "harmonious coexistence" through misjudgments or inaccurate typifications and impair or even sabotage the relationship. An extreme example is "black-and-white thinking," which only knows *good* or *bad* and massively prevents the emergence of creativity.

With the number of different evaluation grids, creativity usually increases, as it is possible to see a current concrete process from different angles or perspectives and interpret it flexibly. Creative people thus stand out through *willingness to change, flexibility*, and *learning*, which, in addition to the assimilation of new knowledge, also presupposes accommodation, i.e., the adaptation of the prevailing evaluation schemes as part of the self-concept to reality. The looser or more unstable the schemes or category systems are, the better the individual copes with inconsistent information and the more creatively they can handle it. However, even the most sophisticated evaluation grids do not necessarily protect against misjudgments, especially in the social milieu. Here, reality is usually different from what normative models would have us believe, which, for example, by applying the "ceteris paribus condition," exclude and disregard a large part of reality. In the case of the "self-fulfilling prophecy" as the most extreme form of (pathological) rigidity and resistance, all attempts at change fail, as the affected persons cannot find their way out of the unfortunate circular path without external help.

Creative people are often good for surprises when they are spontaneous in their reactions. Non-creative people, on the other hand, stand out due to avoidance behavior—caused by their social anxieties. However, all attempts at interpretation or interpretation are also domain-dependent, as it makes a big difference whether a person moves in a familiar environment (e.g., in the family) or in public and presents their concerns. As soon as feelings or emotions are involved, someone behaves unpredictably for other participants or in their own way "creatively."

Stable relationships strive for the model of a "triangular relationship" (with two involved persons and an arbitrary object, e.g., as an opinion about a topic or thing; see Sect. 5.3) for harmony and a state of equilibrium. In addition to many negative behavior forms, as they are known from the various psychotherapeutic schools as mental disorders, those partnerships appear positive that master *metacommunication* in a creative way and can reflect on the relationship itself to heal the relationship if necessary. The key to this is discrimination learning or self-monitoring in the use of positive and negative reinforcers both in oneself and towards others, whether in a couple or communication therapy as a prescribed learning goal or in normal everyday life with daily application.

Creativity in social relationships can best be determined and identified through behavioral observations in the relevant situations. Unfortunately, deficits in creative behavior are likely to be the first to be noticed, so that in creativity diagnostics in interpersonal and interactive relationships, one must primarily assume a "negative diagnosis."

Already during the behavior or problem analysis (e.g., before an upcoming psychotherapy), these behavioral deficits are usually discussed and diagnosed as such. There are, as is well known, many causes for rigid and inflexible behavior in communication or interaction with others, particularly social anxieties that trigger behavioral blockades or avoidance behavior. More in specific situations outside of fixed and familiar relationships, such as in "public life," that is, beyond partnerships or family, a so-called conditional analysis could possibly help further, as it discovers and identifies dependency relationships, for example, within an organization like a service authority or an office, conditioned, for instance, by the structures and hierarchies there, and could suggest a way for the "creative" handling of officials or employees.

Finally, today social media on and over the Internet help to get feedback from all interested users from the social network or community on one's own creative ideas or works and to use this creativity potential in a targeted manner. The resonance can be measured and assessed as a statistical result based on clicks or dwell times.

8.6 Motivation and Dynamics Shape Social Relationships

After the "social cognitions" have been acknowledged as factors that establish or influence relationships, the motivational influences contribute to the "energy supply" and the dramaturgy in social behavior. In social settings, motivational forces become noticeable in different social areas and shape the process. According to the motivational model available for this, in social relationships, it would primarily be attachment motivation, and in the workplace, additionally, achievement motivation and the exercise of power, for example, in hierarchical leadership structures.

Attachment or affiliation motivation is an absolutely natural gift, because no living being, not even humans, likes to be alone, but, as the saying goes, "birds of a feather flock together." Other psychological mechanisms are associated with attachment motivation, such as dependency tendencies, ingratiation or possessive behavior tendencies, conformity pressure, and fear of rejection, as researched in social psychology in connection with attachment motivation. For questions of creativity, it is important how the target person acts towards their fellow humans, because their either sociable or shy behavior is reciprocated in the same way by their contact partners through the existing *"social reciprocity"* in social situations. It is not without reason that social psychological research has focused on the so-called *attachment styles,* in order to identify important personality variables in social relationships that are formative for communication and social behavior.

Willingness to help is undoubtedly initially a question of motivation, where ability or skill must also be added—otherwise, it is said: *"Good intentions are not the same as good execution!"* If liking or sympathy is also added, then the creative possibilities are certainly limitless, because helpful people like to show this behavior and are willing to invest in the relationship.

Undoubtedly, self-interest unleashes creative forces to serve individual egoism and to realize available advantages. *"Healthy egoism"* is natural and normal and typical for social interactions, such as doing business. After all, no one likes to incur losses or, even worse, "be taken for a ride." Incentive motivation and risk tolerance as personality traits that fuel self-interest and steer behavior to one's own advantage must be balanced or settle into a reasonable relationship with each other in concrete behavior or decisions, if excesses or actions or decisions that are later regretted are to be avoided. Greed can, for example, indeed stimulate and unleash creativity, but also act as a poor advisor if, for example, criminal, unlawful actions are later punished with sanctions or penalties. Narcissists or "show-offs" are also creative, who would do anything for their image or self-love and for whom any means would be justified.

In work organization, groups or teams are superior and more productive than individual actors in many respects, as they draw on different talents and abilities and thus exploit synergies. No wonder that group dynamics attracted lively research interest!

"Group hygiene" can also mean conformity or adaptation to a group norm, which is created by the mechanism of *"determination,"* as demonstrated in experimental trials. Involuntary conformity pressure in reference to a social reference norm is not only scientifically proven but also an observable ritual in the practice of social communities.

From group work or team building, not only work techniques but also some well-known creativity techniques have emerged, such as brainstorming. In addition to creativity techniques, which are particularly effective in "creative" professions or fields of activity, such as in an advertising agency, the *"Theme-Centered Interaction (TCI)"* has been offered for the "creative" handling of factual problems (e.g., a reorganization in a company) or social or psychological problems, either for self-experience groups or in seminar form. In TCI, the three elements I, WE, and IT are in a *"triangular relationship"* to each other and ideally strive for a balance or equilibrium. The method of choice in TCI is, on the one hand, the mutual feedback of those present and, on the other hand, the simultaneous experience of one's own and others' experiences in the *"here and now."*

Groups among themselves can use the so-called *social creativity* to their mutual advantage to improve their relationship or cooperation. They then choose the characteristic dimension as their strength in which they are better or superior to the other group, thereby strengthening their self-confidence and group awareness.

8.7 Personality Diagnostics in the Light of Creativity

For the concrete and practical implementation of a creativity or personality diagnostic, it would probably be helpful to have a list of available instruments as relevant personality tests or trait scales at hand! The personality procedures or tests mentioned and listed in Chap. 7 are a selection and recommendation that should certainly be relativized and reviewed for exchange with each new research contribution or procedural development. What remains and is certainly enduring are the personality traits that are most likely related to creativity, whether in a positive supportive sense or in a negative sense when they block and prevent creative behavior.

Much also depends on the purpose of the psychodiagnostics as well as on the target or population group. For it makes a considerable difference whether a selection decision, e.g., among *several* job applicants, or a non-competitive modification decision is to be made, which determines the *individual* suitability for, e.g., a personnel development measure or for another support program (such as rehabilitation after a serious illness or early release from regular imprisonment).

From the known and common personality tests, only the trait "openness to new experiences" from the "Big Five" actually comes into question for creativity diagnostics as a supportive motivational force. Based on the explanations and descriptions, it can be assumed that openness must be fundamentally beneficial and inspiring for creative behavior!

Based on the findings and insights from own studies, e.g., in the context of the construction and validation of the test *"Six & Six"* (see Sect. 7.2.4), the trait complex "approach and avoidance behavior" should by no means be overlooked and ignored for creativity assessments, because creative achievements and behavior ultimately depend on sufficient *self-motivation* (see Sect. 6.3). Newer scale or test developments suggested, in any case, to focus on both incentive-promoting and rather inhibiting personality constructs, such as risk aversion, fear, or (excessive or inappropriate) caution. Creativity is likely to occur and be expected only when certain success experiences are hoped for and possible, *for no one takes any risks without necessity or incentive!* In the absence of "creative success," which cannot be ruled out, the expected risks are very likely to occur, e.g., with an embarrassment or "bad press" in public, which is not exactly image-enhancing but rather embarrassing.

In addition to the already known and included *flexibility* as a personality trait in several personality tests, e.g., in the mentioned use of evaluation schemes or category systems (see also Sect. 4.1), a tendency or positive attitude towards the use of *heuristics* (as so-called thumb rules) when there are no other reliable information for orientation or decision could also be conducive to the emergence of creativity. Likewise, a "healthy optimism" combined with sufficient self-confidence could be motivationally beneficial for the emergence or development of creativity. A new personality test, still in preparation (the *"Six & Six"*; see Sect. 7.2.4), has operationalized these traits and would offer them for testing purposes.

Whether self-descriptions in terms of opinions or views about (one's own) creativity meet or have met the expectations remains initially an open question, as corresponding instruments in the German-speaking area, comparable to those in English (see Sect. 7.3), do not exist to my knowledge. However, it would be conceivable that their use in the course of an extreme group comparison, i.e., between *creative* and *non-creative* individuals, and for item generation could be useful if it succeeds in discriminating these two extreme groups, i.e., separating them based on defined criteria or items.

While every creativity measurement is exposed to the problem of unpredictable and spontaneous behavior, especially in a test situation with controlled conditions, self-descriptions, regardless of which personality area they concern, always have to contend with the problem of "social desirability," which often prevents or questions a reliable and realistic statement.

8.8 Summary and Outlook

In conclusion, it should be noted that creativity diagnostics, whether integrated into personality diagnostics or not, unlike conventional diagnostics through test procedures, only works directly by accepting various difficulties. As has been repeatedly indicated, the problems lie in the incalculable and uncontrollable processes of idea generation and creative behavior, and less in the construction defects of the procedures used.

Therefore, the recommendations in this contribution could be of particular value,

a) to conduct creativity diagnostics more comprehensively within the framework of personality diagnostics and to break free from the dependence on potentially unsuitable creativity tests;
b) to try alternative approaches, such as using "open problems" as a scenario for which the subject has to develop a solution path "creatively," and to accompany and observe this problem-solving process through well-prepared and elaborated grids or schemes;
c) If it does not work positively to determine and evaluate creativity, there remains the possibility to "turn the tables" and search for creativity barriers or negative conditions or prerequisites for creativity.

Creativity thus shares some commonalities with other research disciplines of social psychology, such as studies on leadership and management of groups or organizations. Like creativity processes, leadership processes are not solely dependent on individuals but are highly situation-dependent and do not always function equally everywhere. Besides talent and experiential knowledge as basic prerequisites for creative individuals, creativity can only be observed and determined if, on the one hand, the situation or circumstances are favorable or good (e.g., no external pressure or stress) and, on the other hand, it is personally worthwhile, meaning if the creative person wants to prove something to themselves and benefits from it. The same prerequisites also apply to successful employee leadership according to relevant studies (e.g., according to the results of the "Path-Goal Models").

Some prominent cognitive researchers, such as Daniel Kahneman, have recently rightly pointed out the difference between the *causal understanding* of past events and the making of *speculative predictions* with incomparable approaches and results, which apparently also applies to creativity. Not only conceiving or grasping things or events but also understanding them is both a challenge and possibly an (ambivalent) prerequisite for creative thinkers and actors. On one hand, creatives must be able to handle the available information, which means nothing other than linking it with their prior knowledge to understand it. On the other hand, they must not "stand in their own way" in their considerations or intuitions during their future planning and actions, thinking and acting as usual, thereby limiting themselves. New perspectives and thus new ideas would certainly not arise, for example, in a *"conventional narrow-mindedness"* as a personal handicap.

If the development process is already completed, its result is, of course, available. To understand the process and development, only a retrospective view (or *"Backward Strategy"*) remains. The result of a backward strategy can then, according to current studies, be a revealed algorithm that strings together the events or process variables, like pearls on a string, either based on correlations or causalities, and offers a pattern for future similar events or constellations. Socioeconomic data, for example, collected in mega-databases from countless individuals or households, are today a popular source for constructing these *"algorithms of understanding"* and lend themselves to creative or speculative predictions (e.g., when and if a personal bankruptcy is imminent)! "Savvy forecasters" use the *"Bayes' Theorem"* to optimize their predictions, for example, to update and improve their initially used probability assumptions in light of new experiences. Such a practice would be nothing other than continuous "updating"!

Organizations or companies are known to be less restricted in creativity assessment due to adverse circumstances. It is possible that many company members (leaders as well as employees) are not even aware of the creativity potentials that arise and emerge in the completion of daily work tasks. Occasionally, creative achievements or new ideas also find their way into existing "know-how systems" of "strategic innovation management" for general and productive benefit (e.g., through the establishment of expert systems), so that everyone within a "learning organization" can benefit from it.

Closely related to creativity, resilience is likely to covary, as resilience has the characteristic and task of mobilizing sufficient psychological resources for effective "coping" during or under mental stress or pressure. Someone who possesses these mental and psychological strengths has very good prerequisites for dealing with challenges and problems and successfully overcoming them. In short, or to put it in a nutshell, resilience from a research perspective means an active and autonomous decision to do something for oneself (or for others). From this perspective, a certain "kindred spirit" or a related partial content agreement with some trait facets of creativity is noticeable and recognizable. With resilience, not only are the accompanying positive affects associated with a predominantly optimistic basic mood *salient*, but also the will to be successful and to learn from experiences for the future. Creativity as a facet or part of resilience may actively support this behavior!

If the search for creativity does not lead to success, there remains the engagement with resilience as an alternative. There are also a number of psychometric tests for determining and assessing resilience. However, it should be considered that according to the concepts of resilience research, this construct is rather linked to questions of both physical and mental health care and has not yet been directly associated with creative endeavors or activities as "creative" problem-solving abilities. Nevertheless, both resilience and creativity belong to the attributes of a "successful" way of life.

The investigation of creativity in dealing with social media has already received special impulses. Thus, it can be assumed that creative actors, regardless of their color, will increasingly turn to an interested or anonymous audience in the future to present their creations and to request an assessment of their quality based on the social resonance they receive. In this sense, the creativity of individual individuals (or their creative ideas or works) becomes a social and cultural asset of "public opinion," from which many interested parties would benefit.

Appendix 1

A) Artistic-aesthetic Creativity

Task 1: Designing a garden

- Provide a drawing with property and area for the garden
- Criteria of creativity
  + Number of ideas such as types of plants, trees, etc.
  + Structure such as division into beds, lawns, etc.
  + Consistency (harmony, balance, adaptation to the environment)

Task 2: Furnishing an apartment

- Provide a floor plan of an apartment as a sketch
- Criteria of creativity
  + Room layout (structure)
  + Furnishing (number of ideas)

B) Creativity in Social Situations

Task 1: Inheritance arrangement within the family

- Provide a scenario with heirs and family relationships, inheritance
- Criteria of creativity
  + Problematisation through question structure
  + Regulation proposal with balance of interests and possibly acceptance

H. Wienkamp, *Creativity Diagnostics*, https://doi.org/10.1007/978-3-662-70432-5

Task 2: Problems at the workplace

- Scenario e.g. about interface problems of work areas
- Criteria of creativity
  + Definition of the problem (question structure)
  + Listing of problem areas (categories)
  + Regulation proposal with balance of interests and possibly acceptance

Task 3: Providing first aid in an accident

- Provision: Observation of an accident
- Criteria of creativity
  + Number and systematics of questions for situation clarification (e.g. type of accident)
  + Solution proposal (e.g. first aid, emergency call, etc.)

Appendix 2

The Frequency-Color Test

*The Frequencies:*never rarely sometimes mostly frequently often always

The Colors:

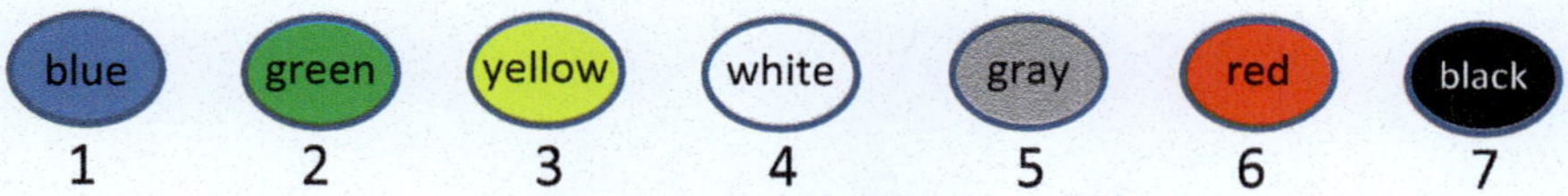

The Task

Please match the frequencies (see table) with the most suitable color (1 to 7)!—Send to: Email address

Thank you

Frequency	Which Color do you prefer?
Never	
Rarely	
Sometimes	
Mostly	
Frequently	
Often	
Always	

Debriefing:

The test is intended to examine to what extent linguistic expressions (such as frequencies) correspond to visual concepts (such as colors).

H. Wienkamp, *Creativity Diagnostics*, https://doi.org/10.1007/978-3-662-70432-5

References

Andresen, B. (2000). Six basic dimensions of personality and a seventh factor of generalized dysfunctional personality: A diathesis system covering all personality disorders. *Neuropsychobiology, 41*, 5–23.

Andresen, B. (2002). *HPI Hamburger Persönlichkeitsinventar. Manual*. Hogrefe.

Barron, F. (1965). The psychology of creativity. *New directions in psychology II* (pp. 1–134). Holt, Rinehart and Winston.

Barron, R. M., & Kenny, D. A. (1986). The moderator-mediator variable distinction in social psychological research: Conceptual, strategic, and statistical considerations. *Journal of Personality and Social Psychology, 51*(6), 1173–1182.

Bartling, G., Echelmeyer, L., Engberding, M., & Krause, R. (1980). *Problemanalyse im therapeutischen Prozess. Leitfaden für die Praxis*. Kohlhammer.

Bartling, G., Echelmeyer, L., & Engberding, M. (2016). *Problemanalyse im psychotherapeutischen Prozess. Leitfaden für die Praxis* (6th revised edn.). Kohlhammer.

Batson, C. D., Ahmad, N., Yin, J., Bedell, S. J., Johnson, J. W., & Templin, C. M. (1999). Two threats to the common good: Self-interested egoism and empathy-induced altruism. *Personality and Social Psychology Bulletin, 25*(3), 3–16.

Baudson, T. G. (2011). Kreativität – Zufall oder harte Arbeit? Ein programmatischer Beitrag. In C. Knopp & O. Steenbuck (Eds.), *Kreativität: Zufall oder harte Arbeit?* Karg – Hefte der Karg-Stiftung (pp. 9–17).

Beghetto, R. A., & Kaufman, J. C. (2022). Theories of creativity. In J. A. Plucker (Ed.), *Creativity & innovation, theory, research, and practice* (2nd edn., pp. 23–36). Routledge.

Bentham, J. (1780/1823). *An introduction to the principles of moral and legislation*. Clarendon.

Bollinger, G. (1981). Kreativitätsmessung durch Tests zum divergenten Denken? *Zeitschrift für Differentielle und Diagnostische Psychologie, 2*(2), 87–106.

Caver, C. S., & White, T. L. (1994). Behavioral inhibition, behavioral activation, and affective responses to impending reward and punishment: The BIS/BAS scales. *Journal of Personality and Social Psychology, 67*(2), 319–333.

Caseras, X., Avila, C., & Torrubia, R. (2003). The measurement of individual differences in behavioral inhibition and approach self-report measures. *Personality and Individual Differences, 34*(6), 999–1013.

von Collani, G., & Herzberg, P. Y. (2003). Eine revidierte Fassung der deutschsprachigen Skala zum Selbstwertgefühl von Rosenberg (Kurzbeitrag). *Zeitschrift für Differentielle und Diagnostische Psychologie, 24*, 3–7.

Corr, P. J. (Ed.). (2008). *The reinforcement sensitivity theory of personality*. Cambridge University Press.

Costa, Jr. P. T., & McCrae, R. R. (1992). Revised NEO Personality Inventory (NEO-PI-R) and NEO Five-Factor Inventory (NEO-FFI). *Professional Manual*. Psychological Assessment Resources.

H. Wienkamp, *Creativity Diagnostics*, https://doi.org/10.1007/978-3-662-70432-5

Cohn, R. (1983). *Von der Psychoanalyse zur themenzentrierten Interaktion: Von der Behandlung einzelner zu einer Pädagogik für alle* (6th edn.). Konzepte der Humanwissenschaften. Klett-Cotta.

Dickinson, Z. C. (1924). *Economic motives. A study in the psychology foundations of economic theory, with some reference to other social sciences.* Harvard Economic Studies (Vol. XXIV). Harvard University Press.

Dow, G. T. (2022). Defining creativity. In J. A. Plucker (Ed.), *Creativity & innovation, theory, research, and practice* (2nd edn, pp. 5–22). Routledge.

Elliot, A. J., & Thrash, T. M. (2002). Approach-avoidance motivation in personality: Approach and avoidance temperaments and goals. *Journal of Personality and Social Psychology, 82*(5), 804–818.

Elliot, A. J., & Thrash, T. M. (2008). Approach and avoidance temperaments. In G. J. Boyle, G. Matthews, & D. H. Saklofske (Eds.), *The SAGE handbook of personality theory and assessment, Vol 1 personality theories and models* (pp. 315–333). SAGE.

Eysenck, H. J. (1970). *The biological basis of personality* (2nd edn.). Thomas.

Eysenck, H. J. (1977). *Kriminalität und Persönlichkeit.* Europaverlag.

Eysenck, H. J., & Eysenck, S. B. G. (1991). *Manual of the Eysenck Personality Scales (EPS Adult).* Hodder and Stoughton.

Facaoaru, C. (1985). *Kreativität in Wissenschaft und Technik. Operationalisierung von Problemlösefähigkeit und kognitiven Stilen.* Huber.

Fechtenhauer, D. (1999). Zur Psychologie des Versicherungsbetruges. In L. Fischer, T. Kutsch, & E. Stephan (Eds.), *Finanzpsychologie* (pp. 188–213). Oldenbourg.

Filipp, S.-H. (Ed.). (1984). *Selbstkonzept-Forschung. Probleme, Befunde, Perspektiven* (2nd edn.). Klett.

Fiske, S. T., & Taylor, S. E. (1991). *Social cognition* (2nd edn.). McGraw-Hill.

Flanagan, J. C. (1954). The critical incident technique. *Psychological Bulletin, 51*, 327–358.

Fyock, C. (2008). *The truth about hiring the best. „Get the best and avoid the rest…“.* Pearson Education.

Glaveanu, V. P. (2022). Social approaches to creativity. In J. A. Plucker (Ed.), *Creativity & innovation, theory, research, and practice* (2nd edn., pp. 37–44). Routledge.

Gniech, G., Oetting, T., & Brohl, M. (1993). *Untersuchungen zur Messung von „Sensation Seeking“.* Bremer Beiträge zur Psychologie, Institut für Psychologie und Kognitionsforschung der Universität Bremen.

Gray, J. A. (1971). *The psychology of fear and stress.* McGraw-Hill.

Gray, J. A. (1987). *The psychology of fear and stress* (2nd edn.). University Press.

Gray, J. A., & McNaughton, N. (2000). *The neuropsychology of anxiety* (2nd edn.). University Press.

Grinberg, L., Langer, M., Rodregue, E. – herausgegeben und eingeleitet von Werner W. Kemper (1971). *Psychoanalytische Gruppentherapie. Praxis und theoretische Grundlagen.* Geist und Psyche. Kindler.

Guilford, J. P. (1950). Creativity. *American Psychologist, 5*, 444–454.

Hathaway, S. R., & McKinley, J. C. (1943/1951). *The minnesota multiphasic personality Inventory manual.* Revised. The Psychological Corporation.

Heckhausen, H. (1963). *Hoffnung und Furcht in der Leistungsmotivation.* Hain.

Heider, F. (1958). *The psychology of interpersonal relations.* Erlbaum.

Hennessey, B. A., & Amabile, T. M. (1988). The conditions of creativity. In R. J. Sternberg (Ed.), *The nature of creativity, contemporary psychological perspectives* (pp. 11–38). Cambridge University Press.

Henriksen, D., Mishra, P., & Torrejon Capurro, C. (2022). A sociocultural perspective on creativity and technology: New synergies for education. In J. A. Plucker (Ed.), *Creativity & Innovation, Theory, research, and practice* (2nd edn., pp. 327–346). Routledge.

Hexel, M. (2004). Validierung der deutschen Version des Attachment Style Questionnaire (ASQ) bei Personen mit und ohne psychiatrische Diagnosen. *Zeitschrift für Klinische Psychologie und Psychotherapie, 33*(2), 79–90.

Higgins, E. T. (1997). Beyond pleasure and pain. *American Psychologist, 52*(12), 1280–1300.

Hofstätter, P. R. (1957/1971). *Gruppendynamik. Kritik der Massenpsychologie.* Durchgesehene und erweiterte Neuauflage. Rowohlt.

Hull, C. L. (1943). *Principles of behavior. An introduction to behavioral theory.* Appelton-Century-Crofts.

Hull, C. L. (1951). *Essentials of behavior.* Yale Press.

Jäger, A. O., Süß, H. M., & Beauducel, A. (1997). *Berliner Intelligenzstruktur-Test (BIS-Test), Form 4.* Hogrefe.

Jonas, K., Stroebe, W., & Hewstone, M. (Eds.). (2014). *Sozialpsychologie* (6th edn.). Springer.

Kahneman, D. (2012). *Schnelles Denken, Langsames Denken* (2nd edn.). Siedler.

Kahneman, D., Sibony, O., & Sunstein, C. R. (2023). *Noise: Was unsere Entscheidungen verzerrt – Und wie wir sie verbessern können.* Pantheon.

Karremans, J. C., & Finkenauer, C. (2014). Affiliation, zwischenmenschliche Anziehung und enge Beziehungen. In K. Jonas, W. Stroebe, & M. Hewstone (Eds.), *Sozialpsychologie* (6th edn., pp. 401–437). Springer.

Kaufman, J. C. (2022). Creativity and mental illness: So many studies. So many scattered conclusions. In J. A. Plucker (Ed.), *Creativity & innovation, theory, research, and practice* (2nd edn., pp. 83–88). Routledge.

König, F. (1986). Kreativitätsdiagnostik als essentieller Bestandteil der Intelligenzdiagnostik. *Diagnostica, 32*(4), 345–357.

Krampen, G., Freilinger, J., & Wilmes, L. (1990). Mehrdimensionale Kreativitätsdiagnostik bei Kindern. *Zeitschrift für Differentielle und Diagnostische Psychologie, 11*(1), 1–15.

Kuhl, J. (2010). *Lehrbuch der Persönlichkeitspsychologie.* Hogrefe.

Landes, M., Steiner, E., & Utz, T. (Eds.). (2022). *Kreativität und Innovation in Organisationen. Impulse aus Innovationsforschung, Management, Kunst und Psychologie.* Springer.

Langmaack, B., & Braune-Krickau, M. (1985). *Wie die Gruppe laufen lernt. Anregungen zum Planen und Leiten von Gruppen.* Beltz.

Lee, K., & Ashton, M. C. (2004). Psychometric properties of the HEXACO personality inventory. *Multivariate Behavioral Research, 39*, 329–358.

Lersch, P. (1938). *Der Aufbau des Charakters.* Barth.

Levine, M., & Manning, R. (2014). Prosoziales Verhalten. In K. Jonas, W. Stroebe, & M. Hewstone (Eds.), *Sozialpsychologie* (6th edn.). Springer.

Linneweh, K. (1984). *Kreatives Denken. Techniken und Organisation produktiver Kreativität* (4th edn.). Gitzel.

Lockwood, P., Jordan, C. H., & Kunda, Z. (2002). Motivation by positive or negative role models: Regulatory focus determines who will best inspire us. *Journal of Personality and Social Psychology, 83*(4), 854–864.

Mandel, A., & Mandel, K. H. (1979). Einübung in Partnerschaft durch Kommunikationstherapie und Verhaltenstherapie. In A. Mandel, K. H. Mandel, E. Stadter, & D. Zimmer (Eds.), *Einübung in Partnerschaft durch Kommunikationstherapie und Verhaltenstherapie, Reihe: Leben lernen 1* (pp. 13–324). Pfeiffer.

Mandel, A., Mandel, K.-H., Stadter, E., & Zimmer, D. (Eds.). (1979). *Einübung in Partnerschaft durch Kommunikationstherapie und Verhaltenstherapie, Reihe: Leben lernen.* Pfeiffer.

McClelland, D. C. (1987). *Human motivation.* Cambridge University Press.

McCrae, R. R., & Costa, Jr. P. T. (1999). A five-factor theory of personality. In L. A. Pervin, & O. P. John (Eds.), *Handbook of personality. Theory and research* (2nd edn., pp. 139–153). Guilford Press.

Meehl, P. E. (1954). *Clinical versus statistical predictions: A theoretical analysis and a review of the evidence.* University of Minnesota Press.

Mehrabian, A., & Ksionsky, S. (1974). *A theory of affiliation.* Lexington.

Miller, D. T. (1999). The norm of self-interest. *American Psychologist, 54*(12), 1053–1060.
Murray, H. A. (1938). *Explorations in personality*. Oxford University Press.
Neves-Pereira, M. S., & Pinheiro, M. A. (Eds.). (2023). *A dialogical approach to creativity*. Palgrave Studies in Creativity and Culture. Palgrave Macmillan.
Nikitin, J., & Freund, A. M. (2010). When wanting and fearing go together: The effect of co-occuring social approach and avoidance motivation on behavior, affect, an cognition. *European Journal of Social Psychology, 40*, 783–804.
Palmer, C. (2016). *Berufsbezogene Kreativitätsdiagnostik. Beschreibung und Messung der personalen Voraussetzungen von Innovationen*. Springer.
Preiser, S. (1976). *Kreativitätsforschung*. Erträge der Forschung, Band 61. Wissenschaftliche Buchgesellschaft.
Pundt, A. (2014). Diagnose berufsbezogener Kreativität – Planung und Gestaltung (DBK-PG). *Zeitschrift für Arbeits- und Organisationspsychologie, 58*(N. F. 32) 2, 95–99.
Qian, M., Plucker, J. A., & Gao, Q. (2022). Creativity assessment. In J. A. Plucker (Ed.), *Creativity & Innovation, Theory, research, and practice* (2nd edn., pp. 229–240). Routledge.
Rammstedt, B., & John, O. P. (2005). Kurzversion des Big Five Inventory (BFI-K): Entwicklung und Validierung eines ökonomischen Inventars zur Erfassung der fünf Faktoren der Persönlichkeit. *Diagnostica, 51*(4), 195–206.
Ruch, W. (1999). Die revidierte Fassung des Eysenck Personality Questionnaire und die Konstruktion des deutschen EPQ-R bzw. EPQ-RK. *Zeitschrift für Differentielle und Diagnostische Psychologie, 20*(1), 1–24.
Schuler, H. & Görlich, Y. (2007). *Kreativität. Ursachen, Messung, Förderung und Umsetzung in Innovation*. Praxis der Personalpsychologie Band 13. Hogrefe.
Schuler, H., Gellerie, P., Winzen, J., & Görlich, Y. (2013). *Diagnose berufsbezogener Kreativität – Planung und Gestaltung (DBK-PG)*. Hogrefe.
Seiffge-Krenke, I. (1974). *Probleme und Ergebnisse der Kreativitätsforschung*. Huber.
Slovic, P., Finucane, B., & Lichtenstein, S. (2009). The affect heuristic. In D. Gilovich, D. Griffin, & D. Kahneman (Eds.), *Heuristics and biases. The psychology of intuitive judgments* (8th edn., pp. 397–420). Cambridge University Press.
Spears, R., & Tausch, N. (2014). Vorurteile und Intergruppenbeziehungen. In K. Jonas, W. Stroebe, & M. Hewstone (Eds.), *Sozialpsychologie* (6th edn., pp. 507–564). Springer.
Sternberg, R. J. (1985). *Beyond IQ. A triarchic theory of human intelligence*. Cambridge University Press.
Strobel, A., Beauducel, A., Debener, S., & Broke, B. (2001). Eine deutschsprachige Version des BIS/BAS-Fragebogens von Carver und White. *Zeitschrift für Diagnostische und Differentielle Psychologie, 22*(3), 216–227.
Tabachnick, B. G., & Fidell, L. S. (2007). *Using Multivariate Statistics* (5th edn.). Pearson.
Tardif, T. Z., & Sternberg, R. J. (1988). What do we know about creativity? In R. J. Sternberg (Ed.), *The nature of creativity, contemporary psychological perspectives* (pp. 429–440). Cambridge.
Torrance, E. P. (1988). The nature of creativity as manifest in its testing. In R. J. Sternberg (Ed.), *The nature of creativity, contemporary psychological perspectives* (pp. 43–75). Cambridge.
Tversky, A., & Kahneman, D. (1974/2008). Judgment under uncertainty. Heuristics and biases. In D. Kahneman, P. Slovic, & A. Tversky (Eds.), *Judgment under uncertainty: Heuristics and biases* (24th edn., pp. 3–20). Cambridge University Press.
Ullrich, R., & Ullrich, R. (1978). *Das Assertiveness-Training-Programm ATP: Einübung von Selbstvertrauen und sozialer Kompetenz. Teil I / Bedingungen und Formen sozialer Schwierigkeiten* (2nd edn.). Leben lernen 22. Pfeiffer.
Ullrich, R., & Ullrich, R. (1980). *Das Assertiveness-Training-Programm ATP: Einübung von Selbstvertrauen und sozialer Kompetenz. Teil II / Selbstsicheres Verhalten – Grundkurs des ATP* (3rd edn.). Leben lernen 22. Pfeiffer.
Ullrich, R., & Ullrich, R. (1982). *Das Assertiveness-Training-Programm ATP: Einübung von Selbstvertrauen und sozialer Kompetenz. Teil II / Selbstsicheres Verhalten – Differenzierte*

Anwendung im Freundeskreis, am Arbeitsplatz, in der Familie (3rd edn.). Leben lernen 22. Pfeiffer.

Urban, K. K. (2011). Möglichkeiten und Grenzen der Kreativitätsdiagnostik. In C. Knopp & O. Steenbuck (Eds.), *Kreativität: Zufall oder harte Arbeit?* Karg – Hefte der Karg-Stiftung (pp. 18–27).

Watzlawick, P. (1983/2010). *Anleitung zum Unglücklichsein* (16th edn.). Piper.

Watzlawick, P., Beavin, J. H., & Jackson, D. D. (1982). *Menschliche Kommunikation. Formen, Störungen, Paradoxien* (6th edn.). Huber.

Webley, P., Cole, M., & Eidjar, O.-P. (2001). The prediction of self-reported and hypothetical tax-evasion: Evidence from England, France and Norway. *Journal of Economic Psychology, 22*, 141–155.

Wewetzer, K.-H. (1984). *Intelligenz und Intelligenzmessung* (2nd edn.). Erträge der Forschung, Band 11. Wissenschaftliche Buchgesellschaft.

Wienkamp, H. (2017). *The influence of incentive motivation and risk tolerance on risky decisions. An empirical study to show how direct effects from these psychological constructs and indirect effects from two mediators connected with risk, influence decision in ambivalent situations*. A thesis submitted for the degree of Ph.D., University of Nicosia, Department of Psychology.

Wienkamp, H. (2020a). The influence of incentive motivation and risk tolerance on risky decisions. *Advance Research in Psychology, 1*(1). https://doi.org/10.46412/001c.13098.

Wienkamp, H. (2020b). *Psychologische Anforderungsanalysen in Theorie und Praxis. Für Führungskräfte und Personalmanager, die Anforderungsprofile erheben wollen*. Essentials. Springer.

Wienkamp, H. (2021a). *Psychologische Anforderungsanalysen. Anforderungsprofile für Management, Arbeit und Business*. Springer.

Wienkamp, H. (2021b). *Psychological requirements in theory and practice. for executives and human resource managers who want to raise requirement profiles*. Essentials and eBook. Springer.

Wienkamp, H. (2022a). *Manipulation als System. Über die bekannten und verborgenen Seiten systematischer Beeinflussungen*. Essentials. Springer.

Wienkamp, H. (2022b). *Strategische Personalbeurteilungen. Wirtschaftspsychologische Systeme für das Performance Management*. Springer.

Wienkamp, H. (2022c). Wen brauchen wir wirklich? Kein Recruiting ohne Anforderungsprofile. *personal manager, 6*(22), 44–47.

Wienkamp, H. (2023a). *Herausforderungen und Strategien der Personalberatung und Personalbetreuung – Aus der wirtschaftspsychologischen Praxis, für die Praxis*. Springer.

Wienkamp, H. (2023b). Manipulation – Oder, „man kann nicht nicht manipulieren!". *people & work 04/23*. .

Wienkamp, H. (2024). *Diagnostik von Manipulationen*. Springer.

Wienkamp, H. (in Vorbereitung). *Persönlichkeitstest über Ihr Business- und Finanzprofil. Der „Six & Six"*. Springer.

The manufacturer's authorised representative in the EU is Springer Nature Customer Service Centre GmbH, Europaplatz 3, 69115 Heidelberg, Germany. If you have any concerns regarding our products, please contact ProductSafety@springernature.com

Printed and bound by CPI Group (UK) Ltd, Croydon, CR0 4YY
30/09/2026
02225578-0002